Erotic Wit

Erotic Wit

Quotations, One-liners and Aphorisms

GERD DE LEY

with translations by
DAVID POTTER

ROBERT HALE · LONDON

Selection © Gerd de Ley 2007
English translations © David Potter 2007
First published in Great Britain 2007

ISBN: 978-0-7090-8354-2

Robert Hale Limited
Clerkenwell House
Clerkenwell Green
London EC1R 0HT

The right of Gerd de Ley to be identified as
author of this work has been asserted by him
in accordance with the Copyright, Designs and
Patents Act 1988

A catalogue record for this book is available from the British Library

2 4 6 8 10 9 7 5 3 1

Printed in Great Britain by
Biddles Limited, King's Lynn

Contents

Acting and the Movies	7
Adultery	8
Advice	14
The Age Thing	25
Animals	28
Birth Control	29
Breasts	31
Chastity	35
Comparisons and Differences	36
Countries and Nationalities	44
Erotic Dictionary	50
Group Sex	80
Homosexuality	82
Incest	85
Masturbation	86
Names	89
Nudity	93
Oral Sex	97
Orgasms	98
The Penis	101
Pornography	102
Pregnancy	104

Prostitution	105
Proverbs	110
Questions …	113
and Answers	118
Rape	120
Sex and Sport	122
The Vagina	123
Variations	125
Virginity	128
Sex Miscellany	129

Acting and the Movies

Making love on camera is such hard work that there is no time for the libido to take over.
Julie Christie
Julie Christie: The Biography, 2000

A starlet is the name for any woman under thirty not actively employed in a brothel.
Ben Hecht
A Child of the Century, 1955

I find the sex scene in *The Tall Guy* extraordinarily embarrassing, even though I wasn't in it.
Rowan Atkinson

Went to see *Don't Look Now*. It was so boring I let my hand wander into the crotch of my companion and his only reaction was the line, 'Any diversion is welcome.'
Kenneth Williams
Acid Drops, 1980

A good actress is always good, but sex appeal is not.
Brigitte Bardot

Kenneth Tynan said I had only two gestures: left hand up, and right hand down. What did he want me to do, bring out my prick?
John Gielgud

They can't censor the gleam in my eye.
Charles Laughton

The best thing about being famous is that it makes it easier to get laid.
Allen Ginsberg
Journals, 1977

The movie business is a combination of a football game and a brothel.
Federico Fellini

These days I get more filth from the TV than from my vacuum cleaner.
Max Tailleur
Soft Drukkies, 1984

She works at Paramount all day and Fox at night.
Mae West
The Wit and Wisdom of Mae West, 1967

Any idiot can get laid when they're famous. That's easy. It's getting laid when you're not famous that takes some talent.
Kevin Bacon

There has always been sex at the movies – only now it's up on the screen too.
Danny Thomas

Adultery

Adultery? Why fool around with hamburger when you can have steak at home?
Paul Newman
The Observer, 11.3.1984

The maximum penalty for bigamy is two mothers-in-law.
Oliver Stainton

Bigamists seldom look capable of getting one woman to marry them, let alone two.
Monica Dickens
My Turn to Make the Tea, 1951

The first breath of adultery is the freest; after it, constraints aping marriage develop.
John Updike
Couples, 1968

If after lovemaking he stays awake, talks tenderly, and promises to call … he is married.
Dorian Yeager

Whereas a woman longs for one man who can satisfy her every want and need, a man longs for every woman who can satisfy his one need.
Jeff Stilson

Tonight I will sleep with my wife, thus making thirty cuckolds in one stroke.
Jacques Ancelot

An intelligent girl knows that she will have more lovers after she is married than before.
Emmanuelle Arsan
L'Anti-vierge Emmanuelle, 1968

As long as I loved my lover I forgave my husband for having a bit on the side.
Marcelle Auclair
Le Mauvais Coeur, 1957

The man who is cheated by an ugly woman has heavier horns than another one.
Willy Birgel

The minute you start fiddling around outside the idea of monogamy, nothing satisfies anymore.
Richard Burton

The first man that can think up a good explanation of how he can be in love with his wife and another woman is going to win that prize they're always giving out in Sweden.
Mary Cecil

Adultery is a stimulant to men, but a sedative to women.
Malcolm de Chazal
Sens Plastique, 1946

I am a monogamist – one at a time.
Hugo Claus
Interview, 1978

I think fidelity is very important. I wouldn't dream of cheating on either of my two lovers.
Yvonne Clausnitzer

The woman who is adulterous in her home must always remember one thing – put the seat down.
William Cole

I never cheat on my wife – she knows!
Maurice Donnay

A lot of men who never cheated on their wives, never satisfied them either.
Gerd de Ley
Houten Dief, 2003

Men don't cheat on women, they mostly cheat on themselves.
Ramòn de Campoamor

When one sleeps with a married woman for some time, there will always come a moment that you take the side of her husband.
Pierre Drieu la Rochelle

A woman's best love letters are always written to the man she is betraying.
Lawrence Durrell
Clea, 1960

I will not cheat on my wife. Because I love my house.
Chas Elstner

What a pity one can't afford a mistress without cheating on your wife.
Georges Feydeau

To be cheated is also a love story.
Robert de Flers
Monsieur Brotonneau, 1914

My husband said he wanted to have a relationship with a redhead, so I dyed my hair.
Jane Fonda

Many a man became a father without his wife's knowledge.
Louis de Funès

I didn't get too many women running after me. It was their husbands who'd be after me.
Charlie George

You cannot be a little unfaithful, just as we cannot be a little pregnant or a little bit dead.
Delphine de Girardin
Lettres Parisiennes, 1843

Extramarital sex is as overrated as premarital sex.
And marital sex, come to think of it.
   Simon Gray
   Two Sundays, 1975

Cuckold's horns are not a comfortable headdress.
   Philippa Gregory
   The Other Boleyn Girl, 2001

I would be perfectly within my rights to kill you – I caught you red-handed with my wife! Consider yourself lucky to have got away with it so lightly!
   Cami
   Les Pensées des boulevardiers, 1994

The three words you don't want to hear, while making love, are 'Honey I'm home.'
   Ken Hammond

Hogamus, higamous
Man is polygamous
Higamus, hogamous
Woman is monogamous.
   William James

Once upon a time there was a faithful husband … oh, that is a beautiful story.
   Once upon a time there was a faithful wife … oh, that is a fairytale!
   Maurice Jeanneret

My wife was in labor with our first child for thirty-two hours and I was faithful to her the whole time.
   Jonathan Katz

He fooled his wife by giving his mistress the same perfume.
   Kees van Kooten and Wim de Bie
   Bescheurkalender, 1980

Unlucky is he who was committed to abide by the Commandment: 'Love thy neighbour as thyself!' and the 'neighbour' he always came into contact with was his neighbour's wife.
Hans Kudszus
Jaworte, Neinworte, 1970

I have often noticed in the theatre that it's only the women that laugh when a man is cheated.
Paul Léautaud
Propos d'un jour, 1947

The worst thing about having a mistress is those two dinners you have to eat.
Oscar Levant
Memoirs of an Amnesiac, 1965

Unfaithfulness manifests itself after the event.
Jan Leyers
Humo, 17.9.1996

If I was ever to seduce another woman, I'd take her husband as well.
Franz Liszt

My husband and I had our best sex during the divorce. It was like cheating on our lawyers.
Priscilla Lopez

I keep telling my wife: 'It's *not* cheating on you with your sister, it's making love to you by proxy.' Some women just don't understand.
Todd Loushine

A woman is a lamentable creature: as soon as she falls in love with someone, her husband is nothing but an idiot.
Jean-Baptiste Louvet
Une année de la vie du chevalier de Faublas, 1787

Some are only good to be cheated. And even then their wives must help them with that.
Georges Feydeau

For some women infidelity is the only thing that links them with their husbands.
Sacha Guitry

Advice

No sex is better than bad sex.
Germaine Greer

You can seduce a man without taking anything off, without even touching him.
Rae Dawn Chong

Never trust a man with a small cock.
Jean Cocteau
En Verve, 1973

The only way to get over someone is to get under someone else.
Dan Cohen
Frasier, 1993

It's okay to laugh in the bedroom so long as you don't point.
Will Durst

The strongest, surest way to the soul is through the flesh.
Mabel Dodge
Lorenzo in Taos, 1932

My advice is: keep the vibrator and recycle the man.
Betty Dodson

The anus is an exit, not an entrance.
Morton Downey Jr.

If sex is good, lots of sex is even better.
Eurydice

If it has tires or testicles, you're going to have trouble with it.
Linda Furney

Fondle the woman in your life once for every thousand times you play with your private parts. That should be just about right.
Barbara Graham

Use your brains as often as your penis.
Paul Kiks
1982

A low-cut dress should not be a self-service counter for the eyes.
Ruth Leuwerik

Lead us not into temptation. Just tell us where it is; we'll find it.
Sam Levenson
You Don't Have to Be in Who's Who to Know What's What, 1980

'Keep them talking,' my mother has told me. 'When a man's mouth is working nothing else works.'
Mary Mackey
McCarthy's List, 1979

Never try to please those that are never satisfied.
Floyd Maxwell

If you're given the choice between money and sex appeal, take the money. As you get older, the money will become your sex appeal.
Katharine Hepburn

If you ladies knew what we were really thinking, you'd never stop slapping us.
Larry Miller

A woman should be a cook in the kitchen, a lady in the drawing-room and a whore in bed. But there's nothing to stop her being a whore in the kitchen, a lady in bed and a cook in the drawing- room.
Michelle Maurois

 Women are like ovens. We need five to fifteen minutes to heat up.
Sandra Bullock

Don't cook. Don't clean. No man will ever make love to a woman because she waxed the linoleum – 'My God, the floor's immaculate. Lie down, you hot bitch.'
Joan Rivers

My momma always said, 'Wear clean underwear when you go out to conquer the world. You never know when you'll be in a car accident.'
Karen Belciglio

When you want to do business with a man, the quickest way is to seduce his wife.
Jean Amadou
Les Pensées, 2003

Never undress in front of an open window, especially not when you're still in the street.
Jean-Claude Carrière
Détails de ce monde, 2004

To bite the forbidden fruit, you don't need to wait until you have false teeth.
Jacques Deval
Afin de vivre bel et bien, 1969

Never make love on a Saturday evening, because if it's raining on Sunday, there's nothing to do.
Sacha Guitry

Never do anything in bed that you can't pronounce.
Mitch Murray
One-Liners for Weddings, 1994

A bit of advice on how to spice up your life: Try washing your privates with that medicated dandruff shampoo, the one that tingles.
Anthony Myers

Don't grab a girl the moment you get into a taxicab. At least wait until the driver puts down the flag.
George Jean Nathan

The only way to have really safe sex is to abstain. From drinking.
Wendy Liebman

Sex is good for slimming.
Julie Newmar

Money gets you laid.
Jack Nicholson

The key to a successful restaurant is dressing girls in degrading clothes.
Michael O'Donoghue

Don't be too clever or we'll scratch your goodies out ... or we'll blow your sillies off.
Yoko Ono

Your dresses should be tight enough to show you're a woman and loose enough to show you're a lady.
Edith Head

The only really firm rule of taste about cross-dressing is that neither sex should ever wear anything they haven't figured out how to go to the bathroom in.
P.J. O'Rourke
Modern Manners, 1989

A man with an erection is in no need of advice.
Samuel Pepys
The Diary of Samuel Pepys, 1660–9

When a woman says to a man, 'You look better without spectacles', then the best response is, 'And without a bra you don't look so bad either.'
Pierre Perret
Les Pensées, 1979

It's better to take your hopes for granted than your underwear for a cup of coffee.
Pierre-Dac
Les Pensées, 1972

The more sexy you make yourself appear, the less sex you'll have.
Miuccia Prada

Every woman needs at least three men: one for sex, one for money and one for fun.
Bess Myerson

You can think clearly only with your clothes on.
Margaret Atwood
The Handmaid's Tale, 1986

Herpes research should not be an undercover operation.
Anthony Cacchillo

I'm scared of sex now. You have to be. You can get something terminal, like a kid.
Wendy Liebman

✭ You can't get Aids from a toilet seat. Unless you sit down before the last guy got up.
Hiram Kasten

Treat every queen like a whore and every whore like a queen.
Anthony Quinn

Never sleep with a girl if you're going to be embarrassed to be seen on the street with her the next day.
Ronald Reagan

Always be nice to hets – they're God's way of making more queers.
Dave Rindos

Avoid the embarrassment of shouting out the wrong name in bed by only having flings with girls who have the same name as your wife.
Viz
Top-Tips, August 2003

If you ever go home with somebody and they don't have books in their house, don't sleep with them.
John Waters

To say 'no' in twelve languages, that's all a woman needs to know.
Sophia Loren

Women should be obscene not heard.
John Lennon
Skywriting by Word of Mouth, 1986

If you can't give up sex, get married and taper off.
Bob Monkhouse
Just Say a Few Words, 1988

Every man needs two women, a quiet homemaker and a thrilling nymph.
Iris Murdoch
The Message to the Planet, 1989

Poor honest sex, like dying, should be a private matter.
Lawrence Durrell
Prospero's Cell, 1945

The purpose of sexual intercourse is to get it over with as long as possible.
Steven Max Singer

Fondling a man's privates is not like testing peaches in the supermarket.
Cynthia Heimel
Sex Tips for Girls, 1983

Never admit to being older than your bra size.
Joan Rivers
The Life and Hard Times of Heidi Abromowitz, 1984

A woman is medicine that must be shaken before, during and after you use it.
Julien de Valckenaere
Flitsen in de duisternis, 1974

There does come a time when you have to put down the menu and enjoy the meal.
Seamus O'Banion

Doctors say it's okay to have sex after a heart attack, provided you close the ambulance door.
Phyllis Diller
Phyllis Diller's Housekeeping Hints, 1966

You don't need a penis to succeed, you just need balls.
Karen Salmansohn

If you use the electric vibrator near water, you will come and go at the same time.
Louise Sammons

Don't look for your real success until you're past fifty. It takes that long to get over the distractions of sex.
Eddie Schwartz

See me. Feel me. Touch me. Pay me.
Barbara Scott

The strongest possible piece of advice I would give to any young woman is: Don't screw around, and don't smoke.
Edwina Currie
The Observer, 3.4.1988

Money is a powerful aphrodisiac. But flowers work almost as well.
Robert A. Heinlein
Time Enough For Love, 1973

The best aphrodisiac for women is eating oysters because if you can swallow oysters, you can swallow anything.
Hattie Hayridge

The best aphrodisiac is your partner.
Bo Coolsaet
Het penseel van de liefde, 1998

No greater aphrodisiac than self-confidence.
Charlie Hauck
Frasier, 1993

If you ask for a doggy bag on a date, you might as well wrap up your genitals too, because you're not going to be needing them.
Jerry Seinfeld
SeinLanguage, 1993

It is better to dream with a woman than to sleep with her.
Hanns-Dietrich von Seydlitz
Aphorismen, 1987

Watch sex. It is the key to success and the trap door to failure.
Michael Shea
Influence, 1988

It's Only Too Late If You Don't Start Now.
Barbara Sher
Book title, 1999

If you come home and he's using your diaphragm for an ashtray, it's over.
Carol Siskind

Start slow and taper off.
Walt Stack

Beware of the man who loves his mother's macaroni and cheese more than he loves sex. Or you. Or anything.
Linda Stasi

Never cross a horse with a loose woman.
John Lennon
Skywriting by Word of Mouth, 1986

If you don't want my peaches, don't shake my tree.
Sharon Stone

Never have your wife in the morning – the day may have something better to offer….
P.V. Taylor

Don't go with girls you'd be ashamed to marry.
John Updike

Never do with your hands what you could do better with your mouth.
Cherry Vanilla

Never miss a chance to have sex or appear on television.
Gore Vidal

If you really want to hurt your parents, and you don't have the nerve to be homosexual, the least you can do is go into the arts.
Kurt Vonnegut
Timequake, 1997

Leave it to a girl to take the fun out of sex discrimination.
Bill Watterson
Calvin and Hobbes, 1989

To talk is better than to caress and make love. To talk. To penetrate each other with words.
Jan van den Weghe
Offerhonden van stro, 1964

Let's forget about the six feet and talk about the seven inches.
Mae West
The Wit and Wisdom of Mae West, 1967

If you can make a woman laugh you can do anything with her.
Nicol Williamson

Remember there's a big difference between kneeling down and bending over.
Frank Zappa

Never underestimate the hazards of a zipper.
Joan Rivers
The Life and Hard Times of Heidi Abromowitz, 1984

Eunuchs unite! – you have nothing to lose.
  Maxim Drabon
  1976

Practice safe sex: go fuck yourself.
  Wim Triesthof
  1973

The way to a man's heart is through his wife's belly.
  Edward Albee
  Who's Afraid of Virginia Woolf?, 1964

Never sleep with a woman whose troubles are worse than your own.
  Nelson Algren
  A Walk on the Wild Side, 1956

Flirt with people at work. You might get a raise, you might get sex – either way, you can't lose.
  Steve Altes
  The Little Book of Bad Business Advice, 1997

Never start before you are ready.
  Juliet Awon-Uibopuu

When in doubt, fuck.
  Giovanni Arpino
  Scent of a Woman, 1992

It is better to be a cuckold than to be blind. At least you can see your colleagues from time to time.
  Guillaume Apollinaire

If you don't want someone to see your breasts – don't take your shirt off.
  Ellen Barkin
  Film Yearbook, 1991

The more flesh you show, the higher up the ladder you go.
Kim Basinger

If it's not fun, you're not doing it right.
Bob Basso

Never despise a bow-legged girl. She may be on pleasure bent.
Billy Bennett

The Age Thing

I'm seventy-eight but I still use a condom when I have sex. I can't take the damp.
Alan Gregory

Now that I'm seventy-eight, I do tantric sex because it's very slow. My favourite position is called the plumber. You stay in all day but nobody comes.
John Mortimer

I have everything I had twenty years ago – except that it is now all lower.
Gypsy Rose Lee

After twenty-seven years of marriage, my wife and I have finally achieved sexual compatibility. Now we get simultaneous headaches.
Clifford Kuhn

At forty a man is past his peak, but a woman is just getting started.
Andreas Burnier
Vrij Nederland, 10.11.1996

I think once people reach the age of forty they should be barred from using the words *girlfriend* or *boyfriend* in reference to someone they're fucking. It's creepy.
George Carlin
Brain Droppings, 1997

The age of a woman doesn't mean a thing.
The best tunes are played on the oldest fiddles.
Sigmund Z. Engel
Newsweek, 4.7.1949

For a man of forty, good conversation is the same as good sex.
Ivan Heylen
Humo, 6.1.2004

Women over thirty are better because they can afford to take some really exotic vacations.
Herbert I. Kavet
Women Over 30 Are Better Because …, 1992

If a young girl of sixteen is seduced it may do her a great deal of harm, but a young man of sixteen is turned into a rent boy.
Lord Longford
The Independent, 19.11.2000

Perhaps at fourteen every boy should be in love with some ideal woman to put on a pedestal and worship. As he grows up, of course, he will put her on a pedestal the better to view her legs.
Barry Norman

I want to die like my father. He died in the sack with a girl of eighteen. He was fifty-seven. I guess he came and went at the same time.
Richard Pryor

Men are past their sexual peak at the age of eighteen. Women don't reach theirs until the age of sixty-four. God, to be sure, had an agreeable sense of humour!
Henry Root
Henry Root's World of Knowledge, 1983

You're old enough to sleep with a man when you don't have to tell your mother.
Nora Seton
The Kitchen Congregation, 2000

One of the advantages of getting older is that I don't actually have to prove my masculinity any more. I'm actually quite happy to say, 'It now takes me all night what I once did all night'.
Dave Allen
Getting Things Done, 2001

I'm going to Iowa for an award. Then I'm appearing at Carnegie Hall, it's sold out. Then I'm sailing to France to be honored by the French government. I'd give it all up for one erection.
Groucho Marx

You are beginning to become old when you are relieved when a girl says 'no'.
Peter Darbo

I'm at the age where food has taken the place of sex in my life. In fact, I've just had a mirror put over my kitchen table.
Rodney Dangerfield

Sex in the sixties is great, but it improves if you pull over to the side of the road.
Johnny Carson

I can definitely confirm that sex does not get better as the years go by and I speak as a well-practised expert. All the jumping and jolting makes sex stupid for anyone to do, but when you get a bit older, it gets to be even more stupid!
Hugo Camps
Humo, 6.1.2004

Old is when your wife says, 'Let's go upstairs and make love,' and you answer, 'Honey, I can't do both.'
Red Buttons

Animals

Cowboys make better lovers: Ask any cow.
Edward Abbey

I draw the line at sex with cows. A horse, on the other hand, I could have sex with because I'd always have a ride home.
Dave Atell

Three reasons sex is better with sheep:
1. They don't waste all that time jabbering at you.
2. Afterwards, you don't have to hold them till they fall asleep.
3. When you're done, you get a nice sweater out of the deal.
Bob Beauchaine

The only sure guide to the sex of a pelican is another pelican.
David Eccles

When I was eight years old my father told me about the birds and the bees. The next day a bee stung me and for seven months I thought I was pregnant.
Barbara George

If you fuck a bull, you get bullshit on your prick.
Paul Goodman

Dogs act exactly the way we would act if we had no shame.
Cynthia Heimel
Sex Tips for Girls, 1983

Cats think about three things: food, sex, and nothing.
Adair Lara
Welcome to Earth, Mom, 1992

Let us pity the turtle doves who only make love in the spring.
Ninon de Lenclos
Lettres, 1870

The copulation
of cats is harrowing; they
are unbearably fond of the moon.
Peter Porter
Preaching to the Converted, 1972

Every animal is sad after mating – except for donkeys and priests.
Ernest J. Renan

Birth Control

'This child received as a gift of God,' said the priest. Nicely put for forgetting to take the pill once.
Harry de Jong
Ze zullen er nog wat van denken, c.1980

Holy Mother we do believe,
That without sin Thou didst conceive;
May we now in Thee believing,
Also sin without conceiving.
  A.P. Herbert

A birth-control pill for men, that's fair. It makes more sense to take the bullets out of the gun than to wear a bulletproof vest.
  Greg Travis

Birth control is a way of avoiding the issue.
  Jasmine Birtles
  A Woman's Little Instruction Book, 1995

He decided to have a vasectomy after a family vote on the matter. His kids voted fifteen to three in favour.
  Max Kauffman

Fill a condom with as much water as possible – then you will realise how small you are.
  Rinus Ferdinandusse
  Stukjes in de kraag, 1965

I've never fucked anyone that was so good it was worth dying for.
  Barbara Miller
  on the necessity of using condoms

A friend of mine confused her valium with her birth control pills – she had fourteen kids but didn't give a shit.
  Joan Rivers

When mom found my diaphragm, I told her it was a bathing cap for my cat.
  Liz Winston

There's a new birth control pill for women. You put it between your knees and keep it there.
  Bill Barner

My husband and I have discovered a foolproof method of birth control. An hour with the kids before bedtime.
   Roseanne Barr

I was on stage last night talking. I said, 'You know the diaphragm is a pain in the ass.' Someone yelled out, 'You are putting it in the wrong way.'
   Carole Montgomery

If my grandparents had known about the contraceptive pill, I might have been an orphan.
   Stan Marcelo
   2006

Birth control pills are taxdeductible, but only if they fail.
   Abigail Van Buren
   The Best of Dear Abby, 1981

I practise birth control, which is being around my sister's children. You want to run right out and ovulate after you play with them for five minutes.
   Brett Butler

Condoms that glow in the dark help avoid nightly screwups.
   Anthony Cacchillo

Breasts

B is for Breasts
Of which ladies have two;
Once prized for the function,
Now for the view.
   Robert Paul Smith
   And Another Thing, 1959

The only reason my feet are so small is because things don't grow well in the shade.
Dolly Parton

Did you see her boob job? You don't wanna drive around in an old Transit just because it's got new headlamps.
Peter Bowker
Blackpool, 2004

While breasts are always a soothing sight, the flaccid penis is not one of nature's most impressive shows.
Martin Scriblerus

For a young actress intelligence is a handicap. She would do well to compensate with a nice low-cut dress.
Roger Vadim

It's amazing in life what we are given. I was given giant tits and a good visual sense.
Tracey Emin

It's called a Wonderbra because when you take it off, the guy is thinking, 'I wonder where her boobs went.'
Rebecca Nell

Males cannot look at breasts and think at the same time.
Dave Barry

Ever since my butcher got breasts, I eat no more meat.
Jacques Klöters

You have to admire the aesthetic taste of Mother Nature – she may well have put breasts on the back of a man.
Amaat Burssens
Het logboekje van de lichtmatroos, 1969

Her breasts filled out the front of her blouse like the humps of a small camel. Not the kind you smoke, but the kind you ride.
Kinky Friedman
Elvis, Jesus and Coca-Cola, 1993

Breast feeding should not be attempted by fathers with hairy chests, since they can make the baby sneeze and give it wind.
Mike Harding
The Armchair Anarchist's Almanac, 1981

As a breastfeeding mother, you're basically just meals on heels.
Kathy Lette

The trouble with finding your perfect soul mate is that she would probably want to get married, then four weeks after the wedding you would meet another perfect soul mate, with larger breasts.
James Knowles

Whoever thought up the word 'Mammogram'? Every time I hear it, I think I'm supposed to put my breast in an envelope and send it to someone.
Jan King

It is of no importance that you are so thin in front, my love! I'm closer to your heart when the bosom is flat.
Louis Bouilhet
Les Dernières Chansons, 1872

If I look at the bosom of a woman, I see double.
Jules Renard
Journal, 1887–1910

My breasts are not actresses.
Liv Ullmann

God gave women two breasts because he gave men two hands.
Léo Campion

This woman shows her tits and she thinks she is offering her heart.
Jules Renard
Journal, 1887–1910

But, you know what life really is? You're born, you suck your mother's tits. You get a little older, you suck your girlfriend's tits. You get married, you suck your wife's tits. That's what life is. Life sucks.
John Ryman

Tits and electric trains are meant for children but men play with them.
Jean Cazalet

Nothing fills a hand better than a woman's breast.
Jean Baudrillard
Memoires froides, 1987

Men who show too much of their intelligence are like women who show too much of their breasts.
Antonio Lobo Antunes

A lot of guys think the larger a woman's breasts are, the less intelligent she is. I think it's the opposite – the larger a woman's breasts are, the less intelligent the men become.
Anita Wise

 Without nipples, breasts would be pointless.
Jody Nathan

When breasts ask to be felt you have to give an immediate response.
Pierre Perret
Les Pensées, 1979

She was a rich girl – breast-fed by caterers.
Bill Scheft

Chastity

'There are worse things than chastity.'
'Yes, lunacy and death.'
Tennessee Williams
The Night of the Iguana, 1964

I do not understand God: first he creates you
And then he wants us to be chaste.
Herman de Coninck
De Lenige Liefde, 1969

Never name your kid 'Chastity', because that's just asking for it.
Meghan Skinner

Chastity is a kind of meanness, the worst of all.
Stendhal
De l'Amour, 1822

Chastity is a virtue. If it lasts too long, it is a sin.
C.J. Casparus
Studeerkamera, 1960

We may eventually come to realize that chastity is no more a virtue than malnutrition.
Alex Comfort
The Joy of Sex, 1986

A woman who was never seduced should not brag about her chastity.
Michel de Montaigne
Essais, 1580

Women are more chaste with their ears than with other parts of their bodies.
Molière

Chastity is meant for ugly women; it is a modern and Christian invention.
Théophile Gautier

Of all sexual deviations chastity is the most unnatural.
Rémy de Gourmont
Promenades philosophiques, 1909

Comparisons and Differences

God created woman and Satan added the accessories.
Geert Bekaert
Oprispingen, June 1982

I've heard it said that sex is like pizza – even when it's bad, it's still good. I guess what I want to know is where I can call to get it delivered within thirty minutes.
Sean M. McAskill

Nobody dies from lack of sex. It's lack of love we die from.
Margaret Atwood
The Handmaid's Tale, 1986

You remember your first mountain in much the same way you remember having your first sexual experience, except that climbing doesn't make as much mess and you don't cry for a week if Ben Nevis forgets to phone next morning.
Muriel Gray
The First Fifty, 1990

Great food is like great sex – the more you have the more you want.
Gael Greene

Food is like sex: when you abstain, even the worst stuff begins to look good.
Beth McCollister

Sex is like air ... not important until you're not getting any.
Debbie Reynolds

Nature is so cruel. When women are drunk, they get horny. When men are drunk, they go limp.
Joeri Cornille

Lawyers and tarts are the two oldest professions in the world. And we aim to please.
John Mortimer

Mistresses and wives are as different as night and day.
Abigail van Buren
The Best of Dear Abby, 1981

Peeping Toms and exhibitionists never get enough of each other.
Gerd de Ley
Houten Dief, 2003

I love hot women and cold coffee: in both cases it means a gain of time.
Léon Zitrone

A man differs in two ways from an animal: he thinks of sex the whole year.
Toon Verhoeven
Terzijde, 1990

Sex is like snow, you never know how many inches you're going to get or how long it will last.
Peter Darbo

Leaving sex to the feminists is like letting your dog vacation at the taxidermist.
Camille Paglia
Sexual Personae, 1990

Life is like a penis. When it's soft you can't beat it and when it's hard you get fucked.
Bill Sadgarden

Sex and socks are not compatible.
Angela Carter

Writing is like making love. Don't worry about the orgasm, just concentrate on the process.
Isabel Allende

As doomed as a virgin on a first date with Rod Stewart.
Richard Curtis
The Vicar of Dibley, 1994

Money, it turned out, was exactly like sex, you thought of nothing else if you didn't have it and thought of other things if you did.
James Baldwin
Nobody Knows My Name, 1961

The difference between a man and a turd is that after you've laid a turd you don't have to hug it.
Julian Barnes
Staring at the Sun, 1986

Digital is like pornography; analog is like actual sex.
Herb Belkin

Books and harlots – footnotes in one are as banknotes in the stockings of the other.
Walter Benjamin
Einbahnstrasse, 1965

✹ Sex is like money – very nice to have but vulgar to talk about.
Tonia Berg
Interview, 1971

In various stages of her life, a woman resembles the continents of the world. From thirteen to eighteen, she's like Africa – virgin territory; from 18 to 30, she's like Asia – hot and exotic; from 30 to 45, she's like America – fully explored and free with her resources; from 45 to 55, she's like Europe – exhausted, but not without places of interest; after 55, she's like Australia – everybody knows it's down there, but nobody much cares.
Al Boliska

Sex without using someone is as difficult as eating without chewing.
Julie Burchill

Trying to keep an affair secret is like trying to sneak dawn past a cockerel.
Abigail van Buren
The Best of Dear Abby, 1981

In love, as in gluttony, pleasure is a matter of the utmost precision.
Italo Calvino

If I was a half as ugly as you, I'd be a poster boy for a prophylactic.
James Carabatsos
Heartbreak Ridge, 1986

Underwear is for a comedy what a gown is for the drama.
Carlo Rim

Alcohol is like love: the first kiss is magic, the second is intimate, the third is routine. After that you just take the girl's clothes off.
Raymond Chandler
The Long Goodbye, 1954

God is in my mind and the devil's in my pants.
Jonathan Winters

When a man talks dirty to a woman, it's sexual harassment. When a woman talks dirty to a man, it's five dollars a minute.
Steven Wright

What he labels sexual, she labels harassment.
Ellen Goodman

Playboy is a lot like *National Geographic*. Both have pictures of places I'm never going to visit.
Don James

Sex is a momentary itch,
Love never lets you go.
Kingsley Amis
An Ever-Fixed Mark, 1967

Where sex is an oasis, love is a desert.
Altan van der Bent

The only thing better than Great Sex ... is Great Coffee!
Stephanie Piro

There's nothing like good food, good wine and a bad girl.
Robin Williams

Food, sex, and liquor create their own appetite.
Sheilah Graham
A State of Heat, 1972

There will be times when your basic abilities are impaired by alcohol. Attempting sex in this state is like trying to play snooker with a piece of rope.
Jeff Green
The A-Z of Living Together, 2002

People always tell when they are hungry or thirsty, never when they are horny.
Charlotte von Mahlsdorf
Ich bin meine eigene frau, 1992

It's just as Christian to go down on your knees for sex as it is for religion.
Larry Flynt

Reading computer manuals without the hardware is as frustrating as reading sex manuals without the software.
Arthur C. Clarke

Surfing on the Internet is like sex; everyone boasts about doing more than they actually do. But in the case of the Internet, it's a lot more.
Tom Fasulo

A human being is a computer's way of making another computer. We are just a computer's sex organs.
David Gerrold

All men, even the most clever, are like Nescafé: ready in an instant.
Franca Rame

Although meant as a compliment, 'You make love like a professional!' isn't always received as such.
Derek Cockram

Lust is when you love what you see. Love is when you lust for what's inside.
Renée Conkle

My aunt, thirty years a feminist, says, 'A car is just an extension of your penis.' Oh, I wish.
Tim Allen

Women make love for love, men make love for lust.
Derrick Harge

Women need a reason to have sex. Men just need a place.
Lowell Ganz & Babaloo Mandel
City Slickers, 1991

Women might be able to fake orgasms. But men can fake whole relationships.
Sharon Stone

It is silly for a woman to go to a male gynecologist. It is like going to an auto mechanic who has never even owned his own car.
Carrie Snow
Comedy Celebration Day, 20.7.1985

Women fuck to love, and men love to fuck.
Carrie Fisher
Surrender the Pink, 1990

Men mistake friendship, but not sex, for love; women mistake sex, but not friendship, for love.
Peter Wastholm

The difference between love and lust is that lust never costs over two hundred dollars.
Johnny Carson

The womb of the earth or a woman's womb, they're more or less the same. The only difference is that in the first one your entire body goes and in the second only a little bit.
Jan Wolkers

Sex in marriage is like medicine. Three times a day for the first week. Then once a day for another week. Then once every three or four days until the condition clears up.
Peter De Vries

I can't help but think that the stronger sex is really the weaker sex because of the weakness of the stronger sex for the weaker sex.
Jody Scott

1830. Poet, take your lute and kiss me.
1982. Poet, grab your flute and fuck me.
Louis Scutenaire
Mes Inscriptions 1945–1963, 1976

When it comes to sex, men can't keep from lying and women can't keep from telling the truth.
Robert W. Krepps
Boys' Night Out, 1962

It's not that chocolates are a substitute for love. Love is a substitute for chocolate. Chocolate is, let's face it, far more reliable than a man.
Miranda Ingram

An old lover is like an old stove: much smoke, little steam.
Aleksander Fredro

Women prefer thirty to forty minutes of foreplay. Men prefer thirty to forty seconds of foreplay. Men consider driving back to her place as part of the foreplay.
Matt Groening

Sex is identical to comedy in that it involves timing.
Phyllis Diller
Phyllis Diller's Housekeeping Hints, 1966

Love is like a set of bagpipes – you never know what to do with your hands.
Ken Dodd

Kids in the back seat cause accidents. Accidents in the back seat cause kids.
Kaz Cooke

In the sex-war, thoughtlessness is the weapon of the male, vindictiveness of the female.
Cyril Connolly

Among men, sex sometimes results in intimacy; among women, intimacy sometimes results in sex.
Barbara Cartland

Love without sex is in any case a lot more problematic than sex without love.
Fernand Auwera
Vliegen in een spinneweb, 2001

Countries and Nationalities

America

An American male is the world's fattest and softest; this might explain why he also loves guns – you can always get your revolver up.
Gore Vidal

In the United States, there are over 25,000 sex phone lines for men. You know how many there are for women? Just three. Apparently for women, if we want someone to talk dirty and nasty to us, we'll just go to work.
Felica Michaels

In the argot of the sub-deb, 'USA' has long ago lost its patriotic meaning. It now stands for 'Universal Sex Appeal'.
Mary Day Winn
Adam's Rib, 1931

Hawaii is a great place to be lei'd.
M. Rose Pierce

The three most common phrases to be heard in Hollywood are: 'The check is in the mail', 'The Jaguar is in the garage', and 'I promise I won't come in your mouth'.
Andrew Yule

Hollywood is out where the sex begins.
Don Herold

In Hollywood is the one place, or business, where the average lesbian does get married to a man.
Diane Murphy

Probably the biggest topics of gossip in Hollywood are who's gay, who's getting divorced and who's had plastic surgery.
Gilda Radner
It's Always Something, 1989

Too much of Hollywood is like a seasoned hooker trying to pass for a knowing virgin.
Rupert Everett

We don't have homos in Texas – live ones, anyway.
Susan Harris
Soap, 1978

Australia

Australian foreplay consists largely of the words 'Are you awake?'
Barry Humphries

Australians are the living proof that aborigines screw kangaroos.
John Freeman

The fantasy of every Australian man is to have two women – one cleaning and the other dusting.
Maureen Murphy

England

England – the only country in the world where the food is more dangerous than sex.
Jackie Mason
The World According to Me!, 1987

A British mother's advice to her daughter on how to survive the wedding night: 'Close your eyes and think of England.'
Pierre Daninos
Les carnets du major Thompson, 1955

We English have sex on the brain. *Not* the best place for it, actually.
Lawrence Harvey

This Englishwoman is so refined
She has no bosom and no behind.
Stevie Smith
A Good Time Was Had by All, 1937

The English really aren't interested in talking to you unless you've been to school or to bed with them.
Nancy Keith

We had a topless lady ventriloquist in Liverpool once. Nobody ever saw her lips move.
Ken Dodd

I don't find English men sexy. They're all queer or kinky. The last Pom I went to bed with said to me, 'Let's pretend you're dead.'
Germaine Greer

It is illegal in England to state in print that a wife can and should derive sexual pleasure from intercourse.
Bertrand Russell
Marriage and Morals, 1929

Have the British become a nation of porn-watching, vibrator-owning exhibitionists, or is it still the land of stiff upper lips? I would have thought the answer was obvious: we're all sex maniacs now.
Cosmo Landesman

She's not dead sir, she's English.
Cathy Hopkins
Girl Chasing – How to Improve Your Game, 1989

An Englishman sucked his Viagra tablet instead of swallowing it. He wound up with a stiff upper lip.
Ken O'Callaghan

Canada

Canadian – a person who knows how to make love in a canoe.
Pierre Berton
My War With the 20th Century, 1965

France

When I was a novice in Paris I saw more tits than nuns.
Pope John XXIII

France is the thriftiest of all nations; to a Frenchman sex provides the most economical way to have fun.
Anita Loos
Kiss Hollywood Good-by, 1974

France is the only place where you can make love in the afternoon without people hammering on your door.
Barbara Cartland
The Guardian, 24.12.1984

Ninety-two per cent of Frenchmen don't know what an orgasm is. The others are dirty swines.
François Cavanna
Les Pensées, 1994

Cannes – the city where you lie on the beach and stare at the stars – or vice versa.
Rex Reed

Ireland

In Ireland a girl has the choice between perpetual virginity and perpetual pregnancy.
George Moore
Epigrams of George Moore, 1923

Italy

Italian men have to make sure you know they've got a penis.
W.H. Auden

Italians are obsessed by two things.
The other one is spaghetti.
Cathérine Deneuve

Russia

Homosexuality in Russia is a crime, and the punishment is seven years in prison, locked up with the other men. There is a three-year waiting list.
   Yakov Smirnoff

Scotland

Premature ejaculation was invented by the Scots, largely as a means for a quicker (and thereby cheaper) evening out.
   Eric Idle

Scotsmen wear kilts because sheep can hear zippers a mile away.
   Blanche Knott

Switzerland

The only interesting thing that can happen in a Swiss bedroom is suffocation by a feather pillow.
   Nunnally Johnson

Wales

Safe sex in North Wales means branding the sheep that kicks.
   Victor Lewis-Smith
   Evening Standard, 21.8.2003

Comparisons

When a French woman is cheated, she will kill her rival; an Italian will kill the unfaithful husband; an English woman will just end the relationship – but they will all find comfort with another man.
   Charles Boyer

After lovemaking, a German woman is practical. She will say, 'Ach, dat vas goot!' A French woman is solicitous. She will say, 'Ah, *mon cheri*, did I please you?' And an English woman will say … 'Feeling better?'
Godfrey Cambridge

The Frenchmen are the gastronomes of love. The English the performers.
Pierre Daninos
Les carnets du major Thompson, 1955

There is hardly any difference between an Englishman with an erection and an impotent Italian.
Frédéric Dard
Les Pensées de San-Antonio, 1996

Erotic Dictionary

A

abortion – the Chinese method of birth control.
Mike Barfield
Dictionary for Our Time, 1996

abstinence – the mother of shameless lust.
Pat Califia
ZG, 1982

act of love – the enjoyment is quite temporary; the cost is quite exorbitant; the position is simply ridiculous.
Philip Dormer Stanhope

adolescence – the age when a girl's voice changes from no to yes.
Joey Adams
Strictly For Laughs, 1981

adultery – the application of democracy to love.
H.L. Mencken
A Mencken Chrestomathy, 1949

—doing the right thing with the wrong person.
Colin Bowles
The Wit's Dictionary, 1984

—what takes so little time and causes so much trouble.
John Barrymore

After-Ski – most men think it means before-bed.
Monique Lacour

Aids – a code name for privacy.
Freek de Jonge
Zo zou ik nog wel uren kunnen doorgaan…, 1995

alimony – billing minus cooing.
Mary Dorsey

amnesia – the condition that enables a woman who has gone through labor to have sex again.
Fran Lebowitz

anatomy – something everyone has, but which looks better on a girl.
Bruce Raeburn

artificial insemination – procreation without recreation.
Rick Bayan
The Cynic's Dictionary, 1995

asthma – a disease that has practically the same symptoms as passion except that with asthma it lasts longer.
Tania Sadgarden

B

baby – nine months' interest on a small deposit.
Brian Johnston

bachelor – a man who prefers to pay parking fees rather than build a garage.
Régine Crespin

bathing suit – a garment cut to see level.
Jacob Braude

beach – a place where a woman goes today when she has nothing to wear.
Milton Berle
Milton Berle's Private Joke File, 1989

Beaujolais – a nice wine that makes women happy when men drink it.
Henry Clos-Jouve

bed – a terrifying place for a man who is not sure who he is.
Jenny James
Male Sexuality: The Atlantic Position, 1985

—a piece of furniture in which you rest while you are alone and in which you get tired when you are with someone.
André Prévot
Petit Dictionnaire à l'usage des Optimistes, 1947

bestiality – a poke in a pig.
Andrew Austin

bigamist – an Italian's description of his last visit to London.
   Johnny Hart

bigamy – one way of avoiding the painful publicity of divorce and the expense of alimony.
   Oliver Herford
   Cupid's Encyclopedia, 1910

—the only crime on the books where two rites make a wrong.
   Bob Hope

birth control – a way of avoiding the issue.
   Louis A. Safian

bisexuality – the natural human condition.
   Lillian Faderman

boob job – the gift that keeps on giving. My ex bought them and my new guy enjoys them.
   Elaine Pelino

brevity – the soul of lingerie.
   Dorothy Parker
   While Rome Burns, 1934

C

cad – the sort of chap who'll enjoy a lady's favours and then announce it to the world by posting off her knickers in a see-through envelope.
   Lionel Marsh

Calcutta – the definition of obscenity.
   Geoffrey Moorhouse

call girl – simply someone who hates poverty more than she hates sin.
   Sydney Biddle Barrows
   Mayflower Madam, 1986

—a girl that works the street by phone.
   Georges-Armand Masson
   L'Amour de Ah! jusqu' Zut!, c.1950

carnival – a decadent form of group sex, but with fancy dress and lots of booze.
   Peter Andriesse
   De Nieuwe Linie, 1.3.1972

castration – a eunuch experience.
   Paul Jennings
   Model Oddlines, 1956

celibacy – the brief period between any two acts of sexual intercourse.
   Mike Barfield
   Dictionary for Our Time, 1996

—a substitute for castration.
   Camille Paglia
   Sexual Personae, 1990

chastitute – the opposite of a prostitute.
   John B. Keane
   The Little Book of John B. Keane, 2000

chastity – the facile ability to keep the legs crossed.
   Colin Bowles
   The Wit's Dictionary, 1984

—the most unnatural of the sexual perversions.
   Aldous Huxley
   Antic Hay, 1923

cheating – two wrong people doing the right thing.
   Milton Berle
   More of the Best of Milton Berle's Private Joke File, 1996

children – nature's very own form of birth control.
   Dave Barry

condoms – devices that should be marketed in three sizes, jumbo, colossal and super-colossal so that men do not have to go in and ask for the small.
Barbara Seaman

conjugal bedroom – the coexistence of brutality and martyrdom.
Karl Kraus
Nachts, 1968

consultant – a man who knows forty-nine ways to make love but doesn't know any women.
James Dent

contraceptive – a pill or gadget that enables a couple to savour the mirth without the birth.
Rick Bayan
The Cynic's Dictionary, 1995

crudités – genitals.
Andy Kirby
New Statesman, 1985

D

dancing – the perpendicular expression of a horizontal desire.
George Bernard Shaw

debris – a foreskin restoration program for Jewish men.
Robert E. Lewis

decent woman – a woman that gives what others sell.
Comtesse Diane
Maximes de la Vie, 1894

décolletage – the only place men want depth in a woman.
Zsa Zsa Gabor

—something that stops where suspicion becomes certainty.
Godfried Bomans
Humor is overwonnen droefheid, 1993

divorce – from the Latin word meaning to rip out a man's genitals through his wallet.
Robin Williams

double rape – when neither party is willing.
Raf Coppens
Nekkanacht, 2002

drive-in movie – wall-to-wall car petting.
M. Rose Pierce

duck – a 75 per cent obscene word.
Lenny Bruce
The Essential Lenny Bruce, 1970

E

easy – an adjective used to describe a woman who has the sexual morals of a man.
Nancy Linn-Desmond

elephant – the only mammal that can masturbate and keep his hands free.
François Cavanna
Les Pensées, 1994

e-mail – male form of headache. 'Darling, not now, I have to check my e-mail, go to bed!'
Leo de Haes
De Morgen, 1.4.1997

erection at will – the moral equivalent of a valid credit card.
Alex Comfort
The Joy of Sex, 1986

erotica – stuff that's meant to be read with one hand.
Carl Manz

—the expensive, legal, respectable class of pornography.
Edmund H. Volkart
The Angel's Dictionary, 1986

eroticism – nothing more than a bit of mucus.
Ingmar Bergman

eunuch – a man who has had his works cut out for him.
Robert Byrne

Eve's leaves – the first mini-skirts.
Hazel M. Beuchat

F

fag – a homosexual gentleman who has just left the room.
Truman Capote

faithful woman – a contradiction in terms.
Pierre Choderlos de Laclos
Les Liaisons Dangéreuses, 1792

fashion – the worst of all prostitutes.
Madeleine Ferron

father – a man who prefers sleep over sex.
Ralph Anderson

feminism – a complaint that is usually cured by regular, satisfying sex.
Jef Geeraerts
Gedachten van een linkse bourgeois, 1977

flirting – can be compared to ladies' lingerie – not very useful but rather nice.
  Wendy van Wanten
  Panorama, 29.3.1991

fuck you – the right answer to the wrong question.
  Gerd de Ley
  Houten Dief, 2003

G

gay people – a people at war inside a society at peace.
  Scott Thompson

genitals – a great distraction to scholarship.
  Malcolm Bradbury
  Cuts, 1987

—the cause of all misery.
  Jeroen Brouwers
  Wie begrijpt ooit wat?, 2001

gigolo – a fee-male.
  Isaac Goldberg

glamour - that indefinable 'something' of a girl with a large bosom.
  Lee Daniel Quinn
  Quinn's Devious Dictionary, 1988

grammar schools – public schools without the sodomy.
  Tony Parsons
  Dispatches from the Front Line of Popular Culture, 1994

guilt – the reason they put the articles in *Playboy*.
  Dennis Miller

H

hair – another name for sex.
  Vidal Sassoon

happily married man – husband with mistress as yet unknown to wife.
  Mike Barfield
  Dictionary for Our Time, 1996

headache – an underestimated means of birth control.
  Rogier van de Ree
  De beste stellingen zijn van hout, 1995

heterosexuality – a boring and horrible lifestyle.
  Edith Massey

homo – the legitimate child of the 'suffragette'.
  Wyndham Lewis
  The Art of Being Ruled, 1926

homogenous – a brilliant gay.
  Stan Kegel

homophobia – the irrational fear that three fags will break into your house and redecorate it against your will.
  Tom Ammiano

homosexuality – God's way of ensuring that the truly gifted aren't burdened with children.
  Sam Austin

honesty – probably the sexiest thing a man can give to a woman.
  Debra Messing

hooker – a working woman commonly despised by people who sell themselves for even less.
  Rick Bayan
  The Cynic's Dictionary, 1995

hot pants – breeches of promise.
   M. Rose Pierce

hymen – little tailless bird. And if you try to give it a tail, it flies away.
   Alexis Piron
   La Métromanie, 1738

hymenopteran – a gynecologist specializing in examination of virgins.
   Bob Dvorak

I

ideal woman – the one who, although faithful, is as nice to you as the one who cheats on you.
   Hervé Bazin

impotence – nature's way of saying, 'No hard feelings'.
   Anonymous
—the most frequent form of denial.
   Yvan Audouard
   Les Pensées, 1991

incest – relations with one's relations.
   Leonard Rossiter
   The Devil's Bedside Book, 1980

innocence – the best aphrodisiac.
   Jean Baudrillard
   Memoires froides, 1987

intellectual – someone who buys *Playboy* and looks at the contents first.
   Jean-Marie Poupart
   C'est pas donné à tout le monde d'avoir une belle mort, 1974

intercourse – a hot pole in a pothole.
   Richard Lederer

interview – alibi to read *Playboy*.
   Gerd de Ley
   Undictated Thoughts, 1999

J

Jewish nymphomaniac – a woman who will make love with a man the same day she has her hair done.
   Maureen Lipman
   How Was it For You?, 1985

K

kilt – an unrivalled garment for fornication and diarrhoea.
   John Masters
   Bugles and A Tiger, 1956

kiss – an application on the top floor for a job in the basement.
   Brian Johnston

L

lady – one who never shows her underwear unintentionally.
   Lillian Day
   Kiss and Tell, 1931

lambada – choreographed sex.
   Joe Baltake

lateral coital position – having a bit on the side.
   Liz Hughes
   Dirty Jokes for Women, 1995

lesbians – sleeping bags with legs.
   Camille Paglia

Lesbos – no man's land.
   Robert Scipion

liberal – one who says that it's all right for an eighteen-year-old girl to perform in a pornographic movie as long as she gets paid the minimum wage.
   Irving Kristol
   Two Cheers for Capitalism, 1978

life – a sexually transmitted terminal condition.
   Walter Pranger

love – more easily made than defined.
   Eric van der Steen
   Alfabêtises, 1969

—just a system for getting someone to call you darling after sex.
   Julian Barnes
   Talking It Over, 1991

—the main ingredient for lasting sex.
   Mort Katz

—stuttering body-language.
   Ludwig Alene
   Cyanuur II, 1962

—the only game that is not called on account of darkness.
   Morris Hirschfield

—the victim's response to the rapist.
   Ty-Grace Atkinson

—a many-splendored pile of steaming crap.
   David Douglas Drummond

—friendship plus sex.
   Havelock Ellis

—nothing but sex misspelled.
Harlan Ellison

—the self-delusion we manufacture to justify the trouble we take to have sex.
Dan Greenburg

—two minutes fifty-two seconds of squishing noises. It shows your mind isn't clicking right.
Johnny Rotten
Daily Mirror, 1983

—what we call the situation which occurs when two people who are sexually compatible discover that they can also tolerate one another in various other circumstances.
Marc Maihueird

M

making love – the sovereign remedy for anguish.
Frédérick Leboyer
Birth without Violence, 1991

male menopause – the time when a man starts turning off the lights for economical rather than romantic reasons.
John Merino

man – simply a woman's way of making another woman.
Naomi Segal

marriage – the cause of adultery.
Léo Campion

—prostitution to one man instead of many.
Angela Carter
Nights at the Circus, 1984

masturbation – the thinking man's television.
Christopher Hampton
The Philanthropist, 1970

—the primary sexual activity of mankind. In the nineteenth century, it was a disease; in the twentieth, it's a cure.
Thomas Szasz
The Second Sin, 1973

men – creatures with two legs and eight hands.
Jayne Mansfield

metrosexual – a heterosexual who is interested in shopping.
Marian Salzman

mind – a woman's most erogenous zone.
Raquel Welch
Colombo's Hollywood, 1979

mistress – something that goes between a mister and a mattress.
Joe E. Lewis

monogamy – never to go to bed with more than one woman at a time.
Gerd de Ley
Houten Dief, 2003

morality – a disease which progresses in three stages: virtue – boredom – syphilis.
Karl Kraus
Nachts, 1968

mothers – women who miscalculate.
Abigail van Buren
The Best of Dear Abby, 1981

multiple orgasm – something like a good stereo – something you see in magazines and which other people have.
Jeremy Hardy
Jeremy Hardy Speaks to the Nation, 1994

N

nanny – someone you employ to care for your children, wash their clothes and entertain their father.
Jasmine Birtles
A Woman's Little Instruction Book, 1995

natural birth – a case of stiff upper labia.
Kathy Lette

Nibelungen – a pornographic work for antisemites.
Simon Carmiggelt
Het klinkt soms wel aardig, 1982

nude skydiving – proof that you can be embarrassed and scared to death at the same time.
John M. Wagner

nudist camp – place where nothing goes on.
Leo Aikman

nudist camps – started by a group of sunbathers who, in their search for a perfect tan, were determined to leave no stern untoned.
Charles Dwelly

nudists – the last people you want to see naked.
David Sedaris

nudity – the best contraceptive for old people.
Phyllis Diller
Phyllis Diller's Housekeeping Hints, 1966

nutcrackers – very tight jeans.
Johan Anthierens
De lange weg tot jezelf, 1977

nymphomaniac – bedseller.
 Hanns-Dietrich von Seydlitz
 Aphorismen, 1987

O

obscene book – just a badly written book. Talent can never be obscene.
 Raymond Poincaré

obscenity – whatever happens to shock some elderly and ignorant magistrate.
 Bertrand Russell
 Look, 1954

oddball – a third testicle.
 Willie Meikle

orgasm – when the ecstatic body grips its heaven, with little sobbing cries.
 E.R. Doods

—just one more thing to add to the average woman's guilt complex.
 Faith Hines
 Ms Murphy's Law, 1984

—momentary death.
 Georges Bataille
 (see also: multiple orgasm)

orgy – fuck-in.
 Gust Gils
 Berichten om bestwil, 1968

outing – a queer self-defence.
 Peter Tatchell

P

paranoia – putting a condom on your vibrator.
Liz Hughes
Dirty Jokes for Women, 1995

passion – a sickness for which the only cure is more of the same.
Gérard de Rohan-Chabot
Définissons, 1944

peeping Tom – a guy who is too lazy to go to the beach.
Henny Youngman
500 All-Time Greatest One-Liners, 1981

penis – a male organ commonly employed in place of the brain.
Chaz Bufe
The American Heretic's Dictionary, 1995

period – the end of a grammatical sentence and the beginning of a woman's sentence.
Cy DeBoer
Take a Woman's Word for It, 1997

perversion – whatever the speaker does not have amongst his sexual preferences.
Julien Vandiest
Bedenkingen en verdenkingen, 1982

perversity – the muse of modern literature.
Susan Sontag

perverted – having sexual preferences similar to one's own, but lacking the discretion to conceal them.
Chaz Bufe
The American Heretic's Dictionary, 1995

platonic friendship – the interval between the introduction and the first kiss.
   Sophie Irene Loeb
   Epigrams of Eve, 1913

platonic love – love from the neck up.
   Thyra Samter Winslow
   Interview, 19.8.1952

—a meal without salt.
   Raoul de la Grasserie
   Les Ironiques, 1911

—a volcano without eruptions.
   André Prévot
   Petit Dictionnaire à l'usage des Optimistes, 1947

platonic lover – a man who holds the eggshells while somebody else eats the omelette.
   Robert Myers
   Funny By Definition, 2000

Playboy – Donald Fuck.
   Toon Verhoeven
   Terzijde, 1990

playboy – a man who comes to work from a different direction every morning.
   L.L. Levinson
   The Left-Handed Dictionary, 1963

playgirl – a heart stimulant for elderly gentlemen.
   Robert Myers
   Funny By Definition, 2000

pornographer – someone who tickles you to death with a fig leaf.
   Luc van Brussel
   Blikken Parade, 1966

pornographic films – nipples cover the screen like acne on a juvenile's forehead.
Stephen Pile

pornography – a two-dimensional substitute for that which the consumer cannot accomplish in three.
Rick Bayan
The Cynic's Dictionary, 1995

—the attempt to insult sex.
D.H. Lawrence
Phoenix, 1936

—one of the branches of literature – science fiction is another – aiming at disorientation, at psychic dislocation.
Susan Sontag

—the erotic interests of your neighbour.
José Artur
Les Pensées, 1993

—a successful attempt to sell sex for more than it's worth.
Quentin Crisp
(see also: real pornography)

power – the ultimate aphrodisiac.
Henry Kissinger
New York Times, 19.1.1971

promiscuous person – someone who is still thinking of sex when you don't anymore.
Philippe Bouvard
Les Pensées, 1991

prostitute – the only honest woman left in America.
Ty-Grace Atkinson

prostitution – a crime without victims.
Suzie Sax
NYPD Blue, 2001

prude – one who is troubled by improper thoughts, as distinguished from the rest of us, who rather enjoy them.
   Babe Webster

puritan – a person who pours righteous indignation into the wrong things.
   G.K. Chesterton

Q

QANTAS – a condom on the penis of progress.
   Ian Tuxworth

R

rape – a conscious process of intimidation by which all men keep all women in a state of fear.
   Susan Brownmiller
   Against Our Will: Men, Women and Rape, 1975

—an act in which the genitals become a weapon.
   Frances Cress Welsing

—the love of speed.
   Benjamin Péret

—burgled love.
   Pierre-Dac
   Les Pensées, 1972
   (see also: double rape)

rapist – a kleptomaniac of sex.
   Sim
   Le Penseur, 1993

real pornography – movies starring Doris Day or any picture of big-breasted girls to illustrate stories on lung cancer.
   Al Alvarez
   1968

rectal exam – that part of the physical examination that illustrates the true meaning of the Yuletide maxim, 'It is better to give than to receive.'
Howard Bennett
The Doctor's Dictionary, 1999

rejection – the greatest aphrodisiac.
Madonna

reporter – something between a whore and a bartender.
Wallace Smith

S

sado-masochism – the employment of chains, handcuffs, whips, blindfolds, bedposts and/or Nazi uniforms as instruments of love.
Rick Bayan
The Cynic's Dictionary, 1995

safe sex – very important. That's why I'm never doing it on a plywood scaffolding again.
Jenny Jones

screwin' around – foolin' around without dinner.
Maurine Dallas Watkins
Chicago, 1927

seduction – often difficult to distinguish from rape. In seduction, the rapist bothers to buy a bottle of wine.
Andrea Dworkin
Letters from a War Zone, 1988

sex – the mathematics urge sublimated.
M.C. Reed

—the bathroom of the mind.
Walter Grootaers
Het Nieuwsblad, 22.1.2005

—the refuge of the mindless.
   Valerie Solanas
   The SCUM Manifesto, 1968

—the currency of the people.
   Pier Paolo Pasolini

—the leading cause of pregnancy.
   Frederica Mathewes-Green
   Policy Review, 1991

—a shortcut to everything.
   Anne Cumming

—a personally encoded communiqué, continually reinvented.
   Julia Hutton
   Good Sex, 1992

—one of the most beautiful, wholesome, and natural things that money can buy.
   Steve Martin

—the biggest nothing of all time.
   Andy Warhol
   From A to B and Back Again, 1975

—one of the nine reasons for reincarnation. The other eight are unimportant.
   Henry Miller
   Big Sur and the Oranges of Hieronymus Bosch, 1957

—the poor man's polo.
   Clifford Odets

—the last refuge of the miserable.
   Quentin Crisp

—a powerful aphrodisiac.
   Keith Waterhouse
   Billy Liar on the Moon, 1975

—just one damp thing after another.
   John S. Crosbie
   The Dictionary of Puns, 1977

—the only frontier open to women who have always lived within the confines of the feminine mystique.
Betty Friedan

—eroticism you can feel.
Eric van der Steen
Alfabêtises, 1969

—love without wings.
Hanns-Dietrich van Seydlitz
Aphorismen, 1987

—the liquid centre of the great New Berry Fruit of Friendship.
Jilly Cooper
Super-Jilly, 1977

—the Tabasco sauce which an adolescent national palate sprinkles on every course in the menu.
Mary Day Winn
Adam's Rib, 1931

—a playground for lonely scientists.
Carl Jung

—man's last desperate stand at superintendency.
Bette Davis
The Lonely Life, 1962

—God's biggest joke on human beings.
Bette Davis

—the laughter of two bodies.
Henry Root
Henry Root's World of Knowledge, 1983

—the great amateur art.
David Cort

—the best form of exercise.
Cary Grant

—the gateway to life.
Frank Harris
My Life and Loves, 1927

—essentially just a matter of good lighting.
   Noel Coward

—the thing that takes up the least amount of time and causes the most amount of trouble.
   John Barrymore

—the invention of a very clever veneral disease.
   David Cronenberg
   Cronenberg on Cronenberg, 1943

—the last important human activity not subject to taxation …
   Russell Baker
   The Sayings of Poor Russell, 1972

—a wonderful experience.
   Especially with another person.
   Dom Irrera

—the expense is damnable, the position is ridiculous, and the pleasure fleeting.
   Samuel Johnson
   A Dictionary of the English Language, 1755

—the most fun you can have without vomiting.
   John Alejandro King

—an activity a bit like asking someone to blow your nose for you.
   Philip Larkin

—the laughter of genius, it's the bathroom of your mind.
   Malcolm McLaren

—a clever imitation of love. It has all the action but none of the plot.
   William Rotsler

—something popular because it's centrally located.
   William Rotsler

—a bodycontact sport. It is safe to watch but more fun to play.
   Thomas Szasz
   The Second Sin, 1973

—the major civilizing force in the world.
Hugh Hefner

—more exciting on the screen and between the pages than between the sheets.
Andy Warhol
From A to B and Back Again, 1975

—a pleasurable exercise in plumbing, but be careful or you'll get yeast in your drain pipe.
Rita Mae Brown

—the most beautiful language two bodies can speak; it is also the ugliest.
Kristien Hemmerechts
Een jaar als (g)een ander, 2003

—discovery.
Fannie Hurst

—a bad thing because it rumples the clothes.
Jacqueline Kennedy
(see also: oral sex, safe sex, unlimited sex)

sex appeal – what a man can only describe with his hands.
Uschi Glas

—the keynote of our whole civilization.
Henri Bergson
Le rire, 1900

—the skill of kindling the fire that burns within a man.
Christine Schuberth

—fifty per cent what you've got and fifty per cent what people think you've got.
Sophia Loren

sex drive – a physical craving that begins in adolescence and ends in marriage.
Robert Byrne

sexit – exit from a brothel.
   Gerd de Ley
   Houten Dief, 2003

sexual drive – the motor memory of previously remembered pleasure.
   Wilhelm Reich

sexual freedom – freedom from having to have sex.
   Jane Wagner

sexual intercourse – a joyous, joyous, joyous, joyous impaling of woman on man's sensual mast.
   Anaïs Nin

sexuality – the lyricism of the mass.
   Charles Baudelaire
   Journaux Intimes, 1949

sexual modesty – an unnatural coldness of constitution.
   Mary Wollstonecraft
   A Vindication of the Rights of Women, 1792

Sexual Revolution – conquest of the last frontier, involving the efficient management and manipulation of reproductive organs for the purpose of establishing the New Puritanism.
   Bernard Rosenberg

silicone – a substance for making mountains out of molehills.
   Colin Bowles
   The Wit's Dictionary, 1984

ski teacher – someone who is mostly occupied with fallen women.
   Markus M. Ronner

sleep – an eight-hour peep show of infantile erotica.
   J.G. Ballard

sperm – a bandit in its pure state.
   E.M. Cioran
   Syllogismes de l'amertume, 1952

sperm donor – the only job for which no woman is or can be qualified.
   Wilma Scott Heide
   NOW Official Biography, 1971

steward – stewardess without tits.
   Luk Wyns
   Vuil Spel, 1993

strip teaser – a woman who puts it down in writhing.
   Robert Myers
   Funny By Definition, 2000

sympathy – between shit and syphilis in the dictionary.
   R. McGinley

T

tabloids – just porn that any kid off the street can go and buy for 50p.
   Holly Valance

teenagers - God's punishment for having sex.
   Patrick Murray

topless bar – a place where you can always find a friendly face – and nobody watching it.
   Joey Adams
   Guaranteed to Make You Laugh!, 1989

transvestites – stalagmites that like to hang around.
   Jan Hyde

—just regular guys, who occasionally like to eat, drink and be Mary.
Joe Joseph

true Irishman – a fellow who would trample over the bodies of twelve naked women to reach a pint of porter.
Sean O'Faolain

U

ugliness – the safest contraceptive.
Hervé Bazin

underlay – missionary position.
Willie Meikle

unlimited sex – the adult's version of owning a candy store.
Earl Pomerantz
Cheers, 1983

V

vagina – hairy toy.
Rudy Kousbroek

verbal seduction – the surest road to actual seduction.
Marya Mannes
But Will It Sell?, 1955–1964

Victorian apartment – place where the bedrooms have only enough space for one tightly bound woman.
Wes Smith

virgin – no man's land.
Karel Jonckheere
Nacht? zei de zon, nooit van gehoord!, 1968

virginity – nothing more than a child's disease.
Frédéric Dard
Les Pensées de San-Antonio, 1996

virility – an illness which is best avoided.
Nicholas Goodison

voluptuous woman – one who has curves in places where some girls don't even have places.
Henny Youngman
500 All-Time Greatest One-Liners, 1981

W

war – menstrual envy.
Ruth Marcozzi

war between the sexes – the only one in which both sides regularly sleep with the enemy.
Quentin Crisp

weaker sex – the kind you have after the kids have worn you out.
John Henry

wedlock – the deep, deep peace of the double bed after the hurly-burly of the *chaise longue*.
Mrs Patrick Campbell
Jennie, 1969

whip – terror for little boys, hope for old men.
Romain Coolus

whore – a mother with a cunt.
Jan Wolkers

woman – a serviceable substitute for masturbation.
Karl Kraus
Nachts, 1968

woman's movie – one where the woman commits adultery all through the picture, and, at the end, her husband begs her to forgive him.
Oscar Levant
Memoirs of an Amnesiac, 1965

writing – one-tenth perspiration and nine-tenths masturbation.
Alan Bennett

Y

yes – the best answer to an indecent proposal.
Yvonne Kroonenberg

Z

zebra – twenty-six sizes larger than an 'A' bra.
Janice Wilson
Reader's Digest, 2003

zoo – the place where your child asks loud questions about the private parts of large mammals.
Joyce Armor
The Dictionary According to Mommy, 1989

Group Sex

Sex with five people at the same time? No, thank you. More than anything, I would find that very confusing.
Els de Pauw
Deng, September 2004

The trouble with orgies is that you have to spend so much time holding your stomach in.
John Mortimer

A threesome was never a fantasy of mine. What, wake up with *two* disappointed ladies in the morning?
Bobcat Goldthwait

Group sex stands or falls with a good referee.
Toon Verhoeven
Terzijde, 1990

Can you imagine lesbian group sex? It would take three girls, two to do it and one to write a folksong about it.
Lea DeLaria
Lea's Book of Rules for the World, 2000

I'm against group sex because I wouldn't know where to put my elbows.
Martin Cruz Smith

One hard and fast rule of my sex life is only one willy in the bed at a time.
A.A. Gill

An orgy looks particularly alluring seen through the mists of righteous indignation.
Malcolm Muggeridge

Home is heaven and orgies are vile
But you need an orgy, once in a while.
Ogden Nash
The Primrose Path, 1935

I could never be comfortable at an orgy. I'd always be thinking there would be someone making rabbit ears behind my back.
Diane Nichols

Wherever I travel, I'm too late. The orgy has moved elsewhere.
Mordecai Richler

Homosexuality

If male homosexuals are called 'gay', then female homosexuals should be called 'ecstatic'.
Shelly Roberts

Most men who are not married by the age of thirty-five are either homosexual or really smart.
Becky Rodenbeck

I long for my baby boy to be a homosexual because homosexuals are so good to their mothers.
Ruth Sansom

Someone asked me if I am gay and I said, 'No, but the boy I'm fucking is.'
Guy Pearce

If a man doesn't look at me when I walk into a room, he's gay.
Kathleen Turner

Homosexuals cannot reproduce, but still you see more of them each year.
Tristan Bernard
Contes, Répliques et Bons Mots, 1964

My parents were in denial about my being gay. I wasn't afraid of the dark, I was afraid of unflattering light.
Bob Smith

My brother is gay and my parents don't care as long as he marries a doctor.
Elayne Boosler

What do you call a man who marries another man?
A vicar.
Benny Hill

There is this illusion that homosexuals only have sex and heterosexuals fall in love.
Boy George

The gay cannibal only liked men.
Gerd de Ley
Houten Dief, 2003

In homosexual sex you know exactly what the other person is feeling, so you are identifying with the other person completely. In heterosexual sex you have no idea what the other person is feeling.
William S. Burroughs

I'm not really a homosexual. I just help them out when they're busy.
Frank Carson

The Air Force pinned a medal on me for killing a man and discharged me for making love to one.
Leonard Matlovich
American sergeant who created a test case to challenge the anti-homosexuality regulations in 1975

I'd like to marry a nice, domesticated homosexual with a fetish for wiping down formica and different vacuum cleaner attachments.
Jenny Éclair

Homosexuals and single women in their thirties have natural bonding: both being accustomed to disappointing their parents and being treated as freaks by society.
Helen Fielding
Bridget Jones's Diary, 1996

Homosexuality is assuredly no advantage, but it is nothing to be ashamed of.
Sigmund Freud

My cousin is an agoraphobic homosexual, which makes it kind of hard for him to come out of the closet.
Bill Kelly

There are nice homosexuals and annoying ones, and the annoying ones want to get married.
Gerrit Komrij
Humo, 10.10.1995

The Bible contains six admonishments to homosexuals and 362 admonishments to heterosexuals. That doesn't mean that God doesn't love heterosexuals. It's just that they need more supervision.
Lynn Lavner

He's handsome. He's kind. He's intelligent.
He's Gay.
Faith Hines
Ms Murphy's Law, 1984

It was a Gay Nineties Party. It was terrible. All the men were gay and all the women were ninety.
Eric Morecambe and Ernie Wise
The Morecambe and Wise Joke Book, 1979

I've just been to New York, and when I went through Immigration they asked me if I was gay. I said, 'No, but I've slept with a lot of guys who are.'
Simon Fanshawe

I don't understand why gay people want to be in the military ... 'cause they only get one outfit to wear.
Kevin Maye

When people have asked me in the past if I'm gay, I've said, 'I'm not gay, but I am festive.'
Sharon Gless

Incest

Incest – in many rural areas in the United States, the most popular form of dating, probably because it's also the cheapest form of dating.
Chaz Bufe
The American Heretic's Dictionary, 1995

Incest is a family passion.
Marcel Duchamp

I have nothing against incest. As long as it stays in the family.
Johan Anthierens
De lange weg tot jezelf, 1977

Incest is all well and good for families that are in good health.
Hugo Claus
Cinema Magazine, 1980

Ever since young men got motor bikes, incest has died out.
Max Frisch

The trouble with incest is that it gets you involved with relatives.
George S. Kaufman

In the country farmers practise incest in order to save their cattle.
Jean Yanne
Pensées, répliques, textes et anecdotes, 1999

I'm a lot like my mom – neither one of us will have sex with my dad.
Dino Londis

Hey, say 'hello' to your mother for me.
Well, that's a bit tricky. You see, I'm my eldest sister's son. So that makes my dad my grandfather and, I guess I'm my own nephew ... so ... oh never mind!
Justus van Oel
Hij is Justus, wij zijn Erik, 1986

Masturbation

Making love may not give you as much pleasure as masturbating, but it is altogether more sociable.
Felix Rexhausen

Don't knock masturbation – it's sex with someone I love.
Woody Allen
Annie Hall, 1977

You know ... if it wasn't for masturbation, I'd be getting no cardiovascular activity at all ... that's low impact.
Steve Altman

The nice thing about masturbation is that you don't have to say anything afterwards.
Milos Forman

Masturbation is always very safe. You not only control the person you're with but you can leave when you want to.
Dudley Moore

✱ When I masturbate, I always buy myself dinner and flowers first, so that I'll feel I haven't used myself.
Neil Mohammed

If you are gay, masturbation is practice.
Steven Moffat
Coupling, 2000

Poets are lovers. Critics are mean, solitary masturbators.
Gwen Harwood
Poems, 1963

What do you call a tall guy who can masturbate ten times in a single day?
No, it's not a joke, I really need to know, because I want to put it on my résumé.
Damon R. Milhem

If music is the food of love, masturbation is a snack between meals.
Steven Moffat
Coupling, 2000

✱ The trouble with the Internet is that it is replacing masturbation as a leisure activity.
Patrick Murray

Sex for sex's sake is no good to me. When I masturbate I really want to feel something for myself.
Peter de Wit
De Morgen, 1.7.2005

Masturbation! The amazing availability of it!
James Joyce

I knew nothing at all about sex and simply thought that masturbation was a unique discovery on my part.
Jeffrey Bernard

The headmaster summoned all the boys who had reached the age of puberty to his study and, after reassuring himself that the door was firmly secured, made the following brief announcement: 'If you touch it, it will fall off.'
Peter Ustinov
Quotable Ustinov, 1995

Acting is like masturbation, one either does it or one doesn't, but one doesn't talk about it.
Eric Portman

Procrastination is a lot like masturbation, it feels good until you realize you're just fucking yourself.
Ryan Shuck

A woman phoned up and said, 'I want to talk to you while masturbating.' I said, 'Wow! How did you know I was masturbating?'
Frank Skinner

The advantage of masturbation is that you can skip foreplay.
Jean Yanne
Pensées, répliques, textes et anecdotes, 1999

I was ashamed of being a lawyer, so now I manually masturbate caged animals for artificial insemination.
Virginia Smith

I'm so paranoid I'm afraid I'll get AIDS from masturbation. So I'm not masturbating any more until I get to know myself better.
Tim Halpern

Names

I bet Leonardo da Vinci was naked when he painted the Mona Lisa. That's the same smirk my wife has when she sees me naked.
Andy Pierson

Copulation was Marilyn Monroe's uncomplicated way of saying thank you.
Nunnally Johnson

Marilyn Monroe was a masturbation-fantasy of bellboys; Grace Kelly of bank executives.
James Dickey

Arnold Schwarzenegger looks like a condom full of walnuts.
Clive James

Tony Blair is only Bill Clinton with his zip done up.
Neil Hamilton
The Times, 5.9.1998

Napoleon kept his hand in his vest because he suffered from stomach problems. Let us thank God he didn't have venereal disease.
Frédéric Dard
Les Pensées de San-Antonio, 1996

Freud was right about penis envy ... he was just wrong about who has it.
Emily Levine

Only time will tell, but I think someday Monica Lewinsky's name will grace the halls of the Groupie Hall of Fame.
Ben Gillihan

I cannot believe the size of Monica Lewinsky's butt. If she does appear in *Playboy*, it will have to be an extra big edition.
Joan Collins
The Times, 21.11.1998

Saying you believe in less government than Bill Clinton is like saying you have had fewer sex partners than Mick Jagger.
Doug Newman

President Clinton celebrated his nineteenth wedding anniversary this year. Bill said he celebrated with a romantic dinner for two and a night in a fancy hotel. Hillary said she just saw a movie.
Jon Stewart

Paula Jones is suing President Clinton for $700,000 for allegedly proposing she perform a sex act on him. In that case, every woman in America is owed millions by construction workers.
Elayne Boosler

There's a new Bill Clinton computer on the market. It has a six inch drive but no memory.
David Letterman

The biggest mistake that Bill Clinton made was not getting Teddy Kennedy to drive Monica Lewinsky home.
Denis Leary

Bill Clinton thinks international affairs means dating girls from out of town.
Tom Clancy

Maybe when Bill Clinton said, 'I did not have sexual relations with that woman, Miss Lewinsky', he was really telling Monica that he hadn't slept with his wife.
Meghan Skinner

Did you sleep with Bill Clinton?
No.
Neither did I.
Small world, isn't it?
Rita Rudner

My Uncle Murray said you're a man when you can make love for as long as it takes to cook a chicken.
David Steinberg

The big difference between the Spice Girls and a porno movie: a porno movie has better music.
Phil Spector

Even Mozart got into music to get pussy.
Steven Tyler

I wouldn't be surprised if finally they discovered that Red Riding Hood was a lesbian and that Snow White had premarital relations with one of the dwarfs.
Ward Ruyslinck
Uitspraken in opspraak, 1971

We wanted to be the Walt Disney of porn.
Andy Warhol
From A to B and Back Again, 1975

Sexual congress in a Mailer novel is always a matter of strenuous endeavor, rather like mountain climbing.
Kate Millett

'What would Jesus do?' may be a good philosophy of life for some, but I find that it rarely helps me decide how much to tip a hooker.
Charles Gulledge

I think Mick Jagger would be astounded and amazed if he realized how to many people he is not a sex symbol.
Angie Bowie

When Ian Dury famously observed that the music biz was all about sex and drugs and rock'n'roll, I don't think he meant the drugs to be Viagra pills.
Richard Morrison
The Times, 13.7.2000

Working for Warner Brothers is like fucking a porcupine. It's a hundred pricks against one.
Wilson Mizner
The Legendary Mizners, 1953

The only thing Madonna will ever do like a virgin is have a baby in a stable by an unknown father.
Bette Midler

Hugh Hefner now has seven girlfriends – one for each day of the week. Someone needs to tell him that those are nurses.
Jay Leno

George Sanders: Jeeves with a hard-on.
Gary Kamiya

Henry VIII, or King Syphilis Gut Bucker Wife Murderer VIII as I prefer to call him, was born in 1491.
Jo Brand

If you have sex with Abi Titmuss and there's no one there to video it does she still make a sound?
Peter Serafinowicz

Paul Johnson's hair looked like an explosion in a pubic hair factory.
Jonathan Miller

Carolus V, Emperor of Rome, was quoted to say that the Hispanic tongue was seemly for converse with God, the French with friends, the German with enemies, and the Italian with the feminine sex.
Mikhail Lomonosov

Working with Sophia Loren was like being bombed with watermelons.
Alan Ladd

Lenny Bruce got arrested for saying cocksucker in the sixties, but Meryl Streep got an Academy Award for saying it in the eighties.
Paul Krassner

Nudity

I only put clothes on so that I'm not naked when I go out shopping.
Julia Roberts

The prettiest dresses are worn to be taken off.
Jean Cocteau
En Verve, 1973

When a man runs naked in public, he is arrested. When a woman does the same, she's applauded.
Gilbert van Aelst

In Sweden, where nudism is a general practice, the suicide rate is alarmingly high. Nudism may be a contributing factor. It's not unlikely that a potential suicide gets very depressed comparing himself with some of the others.
Selma Diamond

People always complain that the only email you ever get is junk email. And yet, every time I log on, I find a mailbox full of messages from naked women who want to talk dirty to me. Junk email, my ass!
Michael Beatie

I worked in strip joints – but I never got my clothes off. People were screaming: 'Don't do it!'
Whoopi Goldberg

String bikinis? How do they work? It looks like women are flossing their own ass.
Howie Mandel

Nudity is not an easy dress to wear.
Jacques Charles

The clothes make the man; the woman is good enough without ... and often better.
Julien de Valckenaere
Flitsen in de duisternis, 1974

If God had meant us to walk around naked, he would never have invented the wicker chair.
Erma Bombeck

If God had intended us to be nudists we would have been born with no clothes on.
Leonard Lyons

A naked woman out of doors is either a sun-worshipper or a rape victim; a man in the same state is either a sexual criminal or a plain lunatic.
Kingsley Amis
The Green Man, 1969

I am not against nudity, but it must be the right side.
Godfried Bomans
Humor is overwonnen droefheid, 1993

I tend to sleep in the nude which isn't a bad thing except for maybe on those long flights.
Bob Monkhouse

'Every beginning is difficult,' said the nudist on a New Year's morning.
Wim Meyles
Spelen met woorden, 1980

I'd like to see a nude opera, because when they hit those high notes, I bet you can really see it in those genitals.
Jack Handey
Deep Thoughts, 1992

A naked body looks ten pounds slimmer in the dark.
Cathy Hamilton
Diet My Arse!, 2001

When you've seen a nude infant doing a backward somersault you know why clothing exists.
Stephen Fry

An elephant seeing a naked man for the first time says, 'You don't mean to tell me you breathe through that?'
Larry Adler

No woman so naked as one you can see to be naked underneath her clothes.
Michael Frayn
Constructions, 1974

A naked woman is soon in love.
Paul Eluard
152 Proverbes mis au goût du jour, 1925

Even the President of the United States sometimes must have to stand naked.
Bob Dylan

On sale due to short-sightedness: villa with a view over a nudist camp.
Coluche
Pensées et anecdotes, 1995

Full-frontal nudity ... has now become accepted by every branch of the theatrical profession with the possible exception of lady accordion-players.
Dennis Norden
You Can't Have Your Kayak and Heat It, 1973

Nothing fits a woman better than nothing.
Maurice Donnay
Les éclaireuses, 1913

What peeves me is that those characters from the 'Love Is ...' comic strip can run around naked, but when I try it, I get sent home early from work.
Doug Rendall

Don't you hate when you travel, and you'll be standing in the middle of your hotel room naked, and the housekeeper comes walking in ... finally?
Tom Shaltry

There is nothing more impenetrable than the shroud of silence with which a naked woman suddenly veils herself.
Alberto Sordi

There are few nudities so objectionable as the naked truth.
Agnes Repplier
Compromises, 1904

When it's Christmas time in the nudist camp it's no fun dressing the tree.
Pierre Légaré
Mots de tête, 2005

Oral Sex

Cunnilingus is next to godliness.
Kali Nichta

The post office announced today that it is going to issue a stamp commemorating prostitution in the United States. It's a ten-cent stamp, but if you want to lick it, it's a quarter.
Chevy Chase

My favourite riposte to a heckler is to say, 'Excuse me, I'm trying to work here. How would you like it if I stood yelling down the alley while you're giving blow jobs to transsexuals?'
Paul Merton

You know the worst thing about oral sex?
The view.
Maureen Lipman
How Was it For You?, 1985

Oral sex makes your day, anal sex makes your hole weak.
  Bill Sadgarden

I'm so against working. I won't even take a blow job.
  Gretchen Cole

I said to my boyfriend Ernie 'Ya gotta kiss me where it smells.' So he drove me to Wapping.
  Bette Midler

Have you heard about the prostitute with a degree in psychology?
She blows your mind.
  Paul Croft

One strand of pubic hair can be stronger than the Atlantic cable.
  Gene Fowler
  Skyline, 1961

I was thinking about this whole impeachment thing, and if oral sex equals impeachment, then I wouldn't mind being impeached, like, four or five times a day. In fact, I wouldn't mind being impeached while I'm writing this.
  Curt Harris

A Jewish guy's idea of oral sex is talking about himself.
  Abby Stein

Orgasms

Why do girls fake orgasms? Because they think we care.
  Bob Geldof

Sometimes an orgasm is better than being on stage. Sometimes being on stage is better than an orgasm.
Mick Jagger

Remembering something at first try is now as good as an orgasm as far as I'm concerned.
Gloria Steinem

Women aren't faking orgasms anymore. They're hiding them. 'I didn't feel anything. Oh that? That was the hiccups.'
Diane Nichols

Fifty per cent of the women in this country are not having orgasms. If that were true of the male population, it would be declared a national emergency.
Margo St James

Every time we make love, my boyfriend keeps telling me to tell him when I'm having a orgasm – which is difficult, 'cause usually when I'm having one, he is not there.
Margo Black

I finally had an orgasm ... and my doctor told me it was the *wrong* kind.
Woody Allen
Manhattan, 1979

Eighty years ago orgasms were not allowed for women – they were branded as wicked.
Nowadays they have to have orgasms or they are not fit to be mistresses.
Ariane Amsberg
Nieuwe Revu, 1983

My wife's been faking her orgasms – in front of my friends.
Tony Daro

If only the woman's orgasms led to pregnancy, then the whole world would be underpopulated.
Amanda Marteleur

In the case of some women, orgasms take a bit of time. Before signing on to a partner, make sure you are willing to lay aside, say, the month of June, with sandwiches having to be brought in.
Bruce J. Friedman
Sex and the Lonely Guy, 1977

Man and wife know nothing of each other's orgasms.
A.F.Th. van der Heijden
Vallende ouders, 1983

The walls of my apartment are so thin that when my neighbours have sex, I have an orgasm.
Linda Herskovic

Girls can have orgasms 100 per cent of the time, but only when they're on their own.
Cathy Hopkins
Girl Chasing – How to Improve Your Game, 1989

Men can't fake orgasms. That's why they fake commitments.
Diana Jordan and Paul Seaburn
A Wife's Little Instruction Book, 1994

The orgasm has replaced the cross as the focus of longing and fulfilment.
Malcolm Muggeridge

Women used to have time to make mince pies and had to fake orgasms. Now we can manage the orgasms, but we have to fake the mince pies.
Allison Pearson

Sometimes men yell, 'I'm coming, I'm coming.'
I'm not going anywhere.
I think maybe they think I don't know what's going on. Then I think I'm not in bed with them as a partner. I'm there as a witness.
  Emily Levine

The Penis

In our culture, if you don't have a penis, the only true contribution you can make is to lose twenty pounds.
  Tyne Daly

My 3-year-old is so enamored of his penis these days that he can't do anything that requires two hands.
  Molly Ryan

Of course size matters. Whoever says it doesn't matter is just a liar with a small dick.
  Pamela Anderson

A man is two people, himself and his cock. A man always takes his friend to the party. Of the two, the friend is the nicer, being more able to show his feelings.
  Beryl Bainbridge

God gave men a penis and a brain, but not enough blood to use both at the same time.
  Anne Fine
  Mrs Doubtfire, 1993

Few men can make a living from their penis – combining work with pleasure.
J.W. Holsbergen
Wimpie de naaidoos, 1971

After lovemaking the penis is about as much use as vinyl wallpaper in a dog-kennel.
Erika Jenninger

The penis is obviously going the way of the veriform appendix.
Jill Johnston

I like my penis, but I do not think it requires boldface, capitalization, italics, or other forms of typographical emphasis.
Eugene Bild

The only time you ever see a penis in the movies is if a pervert sits down next to you.
Elayne Boosler

I said to my doctor the other day, 'My penis is burning.' He said, 'That's just because someone is talking about it.'
Garry Shandling

Pornography

Pornography is a more civilized version of rape. That is to say, it is an appeal to the masculine desire to conquer and penetrate without personal involvement.
Colin Wilson
The Sexual Dimension in Literature, 1982

A widespread taste for pornography means that nature is alerting us to some threat of extinction.
J.G. Ballard

You're never disappointed in an X-rated movie. You don't say, 'Gee, I never thought it would end that way.'
Richard Jeni

My reaction to porno films is as follows: After the first ten minutes, I want to go home and screw. After the first twenty minutes, I never want to screw again as long as I live.
Erica Jong
Fear of Flying, 1973

Sorry I'm late for the meeting but I got stuck in a porn site on the Internet and had to spend five hours going through every page before I managed to get out.
Jasmine Birtles
A Little Book of Excuses, 2001

I don't think pornography is very harmful, but it is terribly, terribly boring.
Noel Coward
The Observer, 24.9.1972

Pornography is the theory, and rape is the practice.
Robin Morgan
Going Too Far: the Personal Chronicle of a Feminist, 1978

No one ever died from an overdose of pornography.
William Margold

To men, porno movies are beautiful love stories with all the boring stuff taken out.
Richard Jeni

Pregnancy

Teenage girls can get pregnant merely by standing downwind of teenage boys.
   Dave Barry

I wish I could stay longer, but my girlfriend's getting pregnant tonight and I'd like to be there when it happens.
   Teddy Bergeron

The bride was pregnant, so everyone threw puffed rice.
   Dick Cavett

Love – it's all fun and games till someone loses an eye or gets pregnant.
   Jim Cole

To my neighbour's pregnant wife:
Sorry!
   Herman Finkers
   Ik Jan Klaassen, 1993

Yankee men are so lazy they marry pregnant women.
   Lewis Grizzard
   The Wit and Wisdom of Lewis Grizzard, 1993

One good thing about having a girlfriend in prison is that you never have to worry about getting her pregnant.
   Dave Henry

Men are always flabbergasted when the girl gets pregnant.
   Faith Hines
   Ms Murphy's Law, 1984

She didn't mean to get pregnant. It was a cock-up.
   Robert Kilroy-Silk

I didn't know how babies were made until I was pregnant with my fourth child.
   Loretta Lynn

I'm pregnant. No need to applaud; I was asleep at the time.
   Jeanne McBride

The price to pay for teenage sex is pretty high – unwanted pregnancy, disease, and ending up with one ear bigger than the other because it's always cocked toward the front door in case the parents come home early.
   Michael Moore
   Dude, Where's My Country?, 2003

Prostitution

And finally, I think we should keep prostitutes off our city streets. I do the best I can every night. But I'm just one guy.
   Dino Londis

There was a time when I thought that an 'escort service' was a maintenance programme for a Ford Escort.
   Geert Hoste
   Dag Allemaal, 27.4.2004

A temperance hotel! You might as well talk about a celibate brothel.
   George Tyrrell

I never thought of myself as a wicked brothel-keeper. I thought of myself as a welfare worker.
Cynthia Payne

Prostitutes for pleasure, concubines for service, wives for breeding and a melon for ecstasy.
Richard Burton

A successful prostitute is better than a misled saint.
Nawal El Saadawi
Woman at Point Zero, 1983

It is better to have loved and lost than to have paid for it and not liked it.
Hiram Kasten

Women: you can't live with them; you can't live without them. That's probably why you can rent one for the evening.
Jim Stark

You know what I like about hookers? It doesn't matter what line you use on them, because they all work.
Kip Addotta

It is nice to make a job of your hobby, said the prostitute.
Johan Anthierens
De lange weg tot jezelf, 1977

Marriage or brothel: 'No money, no buttocks.'
Honoré de Balzac
Pensées, Sujets, Fragments, 1833

You are always so negative. You come up with far more 'cons' than 'pros'. Surely there's something you are 'pro'.
No, there isn't. Well, actually, come to think of it I am pro stitution....
Gerd de Ley
Houten Dief, 2003

Wouldn't it be great if hookers accepted credit cards, just like gas stations?
That way, if you were in a hurry you could use the convenient pay-at-the-pimp feature.
   Kim Moser

My sister claimed sexual harassment on the job, which was a little bit surprising, since she's a hooker.
   George Miller

There's a little bit of hooker in every woman. A little bit of hooker and a little bit of God.
   Sarah Miles

I'm staying in a strange hotel. I called room service for a sandwich and they sent up two hookers.
   Bill Maher

Statistically ... you have more chance of contracting Aids from a Catholic priest than from a prostitute.
   Nina Lopez-Jones
   The Independent, 13.9.1992

Man is measured by the extent of his patience, except in a brothel.
   P.V. Loosjes
   Maatstaf, September 1963

A prostitute once told me that there is more dignity in waiting for men than in running after them.
   Jules Lemaître

If a woman hasn't got a tiny streak of harlot in her, she is a dry stick as a rule.
   D.H. Lawrence

It is hard work and great art to make life not so serious. Prostitutes know this too.
   John Irving
   The Hotel New Hampshire, 1981

What do prostitutes do at a convention when they let their hair down? Do they wear flat shoes and stand up a lot?
Roseanne Barr

Prostitution gives her an opportunity to meet people. It provides fresh air and wholesome exercise, and it keeps her out of trouble.
Joseph Heller
Catch 22, 1961

When a man has a lot of mistresses, they call him a Don Juan. When a woman has a lot of lovers, they call her a whore.
Brigitte Bardot

Lust in women is a matter of intelligence. Therefore all whores are stupid.
Harry Mulisch
Vergrote Raadsels, 1994

You don't pay for sex, you pay him/her to leave after you're done.
Ryan Shuck

The woman who gets paid for her love, sells something she doesn't possess.
A. Basta
Bribes, 1836

All women can be bought, except some prostitutes.
Philippe Bouvard
Maximes au minimum, 1984

I've made so many movies playing a hooker that they don't pay me in the regular way any more. They leave it on the dresser.
Shirley MacLaine
Out on a Limb, 1983

Just one day of being a minister or a prostitute gives you the right to that title for the rest of your life.
César Campinchi

Prostitutes have a great therapeutic value.
Maureen Colquhoun
The Observer, 11.3.1979

Gentleman of standing don't go to the whores.
They marry them.
Patrick Conrad
De Morgen, 30.12.1988

Notice seen in a brothel:
THE MANAGEMENT REGRETS THAT IT IS NOT PERMITTED IN THIS ESTABLISHMENT TO SCREW WOMEN YOU HAVE BROUGHT IN YOURSELVES.
Gust Gils
Berichten om bestwil, 1968

The big difference between sex for money and sex for free is that sex for money usually costs a lot less.
Brendan Francis

What most men desire is a virgin who is a whore.
Edward Dahlberg
Reasons of the Heart, 1965

Sex is hardly a fitting subject for the dinner table. Except perhaps a table at a brothel.
Richard Curtis
Blackadder, 1986

Good taste and humour are a contradiction in terms, like a chaste whore.
Malcolm Muggeridge
Time, 14.9.1953

You can lead a horticulture, but you can't make her think.
Dorothy Parker

Proverbs

* One orgasm in the bush is worth two in the hand.
Robert Reisner

Pornography is in the groin of the beholder.
Charles Rembar
The End of Obscenity, 1968

Too many cooks spoil the brothel.
Polly Adler
A House Is Not a Home, 1954

In the land of the eunuchs a one-balled man is king.
Lieven Andries

A thing of beauty is a copulation for ever.
Roland Bergen

Better one pill in the hand, than nine months in the air.
Peter Mielants
One Man Show, 1969

Better a laying hen than an impotent rooster.
Koen van Meel

Tell me with whom you sleep and I'll tell you about whom you dream.
Stanislaw Jerzy Lec
Unkempt Thoughts, 1962

Sex, unlike justice, should not be seen to be done.
Evelyn Laye

Save a mouse, eat a pussy.
Kevin Peter Kelly

Sin now, pray later.
Bruce Lansky

Better once too many than once too few.
Walter Kempowski
Tadellöser & Wolff, 1978

To climb Mount Venus everybody uses his best stick.
Karel Jonckheere
Nacht? zei de zon, nooit van gehoord!, 1968

When the prick stands up the brains get buried in the ground.
Virginia Ironside
Made for Each Other, 1985

Better one dick in the hand, than the air of ten.
Rob van Houten

Underneath every successful man there is a woman.
Liz Hughes
Dirty Jokes for Women, 1995

If at first you don't succeed, keep on sucking till you do succeed!
Curly Howard

When the stocks go up, the cocks go up.
Xaviera Hollander

It is better to copulate than never.
Robert A. Heinlein

Coïto, ergo sum.
   Randall Garrett

You have to hit a woman while she is hot.
   Jean Fayard
   Le mal d'amour, 1931

A dirty mind is a joy forever.
   Lew Epstein

He who can, fucks;
the others flirt.
   Georges Elgozy
   Le contradictionnaire ou l'esprit des mots, 1967

Afterthought on de Sade's view of sexual enjoyment: a pleasure shared is a pleasure halved.
   Kenneth Tynan
   The Diaries of Kenneth Tynan, 2000

Show me a low cut dress and I'll show you a cold shoulder.
   Dave Coble

You fuck more flies with vaseline than with vinegar.
   Professor Choron

In the beginning there was the penis.
   Blaise Cendrars
   Emmène-moi au bout du monde, 1955

One man's wife is another man's happiness.
   Gustave Flaubert

If at first you don't succeed ... try her with another vodka and bitter lemon.
   Mitch Murray
   One-Liners for Business, 1997

Where there is a willy, there is a way.
   Gerd de Ley
   Undictated Thoughts, 1999

 An orgasm a day keeps the doctor away.
   Mae West
   The Wit and Wisdom of Mae West, 1967

All roads lead to Sodom.
   Evelyn Waugh

Questions

Nice guys finish last. What's wrong with that? Isn't that what most women want?
   Bob Ettinger

In the last couple of weeks I have seen the ads for the Wonderbra. Is that really a problem in this country? Men not paying enough attention to women's breasts?
   Hugh Grant

Why did God give us genitals then if he wanted us to think clearly?
   Graham Greene

Remember when 'safe sex' meant your parents had gone away for the weekend?
   Rhonda Hansome

Did God invent alcohol so ugly people can have sex too?
   Michael Powell
   Dumb Questions, 2001

If it's really such a Wonderful Life, why can't I get laid?
Anderson Reggio

Of course men have names for their penis. Would you want to be bossed around by someone you don't even know?
Maggie Paley

Is sexual harassment at work a problem for the self-employed?
Victoria Wood
One-Woman Show, 1984

Why is it that a woman will scratch a dog's belly but won't scratch her man's?
Lewis Grizzard
The Wit and Wisdom of Lewis Grizzard, 1993

We weren't making love, we were horizontally networking. Don't you know *anything* about e-commerce?
Jasmine Birtles
A Little Book of Excuses, 2001

What do hookers do on their night off, type?
Elayne Boosler

What I wanta know is, if we're so oversexed, how come we're still a minority?
Flip Wilson

Some people say older men have long endurance and can make love longer. Let's think about this. Who wants to fuck an old man for a long time?
Marsha Warfield

Would lesbians still be lesbians if there were no men?
Paul Walker

Hey, mother,
if you raffle your daughter,
do I get a ticket?
C.B. Vaandrager
Gard Sivik, 1964

Who is this Greek chap Clitoris they're talking about?
Lord Albermarle

The human desire for food and sex is relatively equal. If there are armed rapes why should there not be armed hot dog thefts?
John Kennedy Toole
A Confederacy of Dunces, 1980

Ever heard of a boy asking a girl: 'May I stroke your doggie?'
GodeLiva Uleners

Some condom packages are stamped 'Reservoir'. You mean those things can generate hydroelectric power?
Elayne Boosler

If sex is so personal, why are we expected to share it with someone else?
Lily Tomlin

Every year we have one more million Chinese.
Do Chinese women never have a headache?
Max Tailleur
Soft Drukkies, 1984

If a man is pictured chopping off a woman's breast, it only gets an R rating, but if, God forbid, a man is pictured kissing a woman's breast, it gets an X rating. Why is violence more acceptable than tenderness?
Sally Struthers

What do you give the man who's had everyone?
Alana Stewart

Why is brassière singular and panties plural?
Bill Sadgarden

Does this condom make me look fat?
Maxim Drabon

If there were no husbands, who would look after our mistresses?
George Moore
Epigrams of George Moore, 1923

The shortest are the best.
Is that the word of a sexologist?
Pierre-Robert Leclercq
Mes Catins, Les Belles Lettres, Paris 2005

Aren't women prudes if they don't and prostitutes if they do?
Kate Millett
Speech, 22.3.1975

'Please, I'll only put it in for a minute.'
She replies with 'What does he think I am, a microwave?'
Beverly Mickins

My sister didn't have such a good day. She's asthmatic and in the middle of an attack she got an obscene phone call. The guy on the other end said, 'Did I call you or did you call me?'
John Mendoza

Isn't it interesting how the sounds are the same for an awful nightmare and great sex?
Rue McClanahan

Religion, aristocracy, sex and mystery ... Christ, said the Duchess, I'm pregnant. Whodunnit?
W. Somerset Maugham
A Writer's Notebook, 1949

If you've got Aids, you can come into this country. If you've got fruit, you can't. Do you understand this?
Jackie Mason
Jackie Mason's America, 1983

Can you picture Joan of Arc in see-through pyjamas?
Arthur Marshall
Sunny Side Up, 1988

Is it blasphemy if when you die, you have your scrotch cremated and spread over the Virgin Islands?
Bruce Baum

But if God had wanted us to think with our wombs, why did He give us a brain?
Clare Boothe Luce
Slam the Door Softly, 1970

Can there be a more intimate communication between two beings than copulation?
Georges Simenon

Why do most forms of swearing involve deities or genitals?
Jerry Seinfeld
SeinLanguage, 1993

Why do men have nipples?
Silver Rose
Women Who Joke Too Much, 1995

Why the hell should I get a wife when the man next door's got one?
Furry Lewis

If you were a bloke, would you put it in a mouth where there are teeth? The teeth of a female who's been discriminated against for centuries?
Kathy Lette

Are naked women intelligent?
Stanislaw Jerzy Lec
Unkempt Thoughts, 1962

And Answers

What's the difference between being black and being gay?
When you're black, you don't have to tell your parents.
Pieter-Dirk Uys

What does the receptionist at the sperm clinic say to clients as they are leaving?
Thanks for coming.
Sandra Wilson

What's the height of conceit?
Having an orgasm and calling out your own name.
Teresa Berus

What do electric train sets and women's breasts have in common? They were both originally intended for children but it's the fathers that play with them.
Terry Galen

If I were asked for a one line answer to the question 'What makes a woman good in bed?' I would say, 'A man who is good in bed.'
Bob Guccione

If your wife ever asks, 'Is that a twinkle I see in your eye tonight, dear?', it's not a good thing to answer, 'No, it's prob-

ably just a piece of glitter from the dress that hooker was wearing.
Rolf Lundgren

You know 'that look' women get when they want sex? Me neither.
Steve Martin

'Is anything worn beneath the kilt?'
'No, it's all in perfect working order!'
Spike Milligan
The Great McGonagall Scrapbook, 1975

How would I rank sex, smoking and vodka in order of preference? All three at once.
Kate Moss

Do you know the difference between 'Aaah' and 'Oooh'? The answer: about five centimetres.
Coluche
Pensées et anecdotes, 1995

What do a Christmas tree and a priest have in common?
Their balls are just for decoration.
Graham Norton

Why don't posh girls go to orgies?
Because there are too many thank-you letters to write.
Joy Persaud

What was the name of the little boy whose nuts grew every time he told a lie?
Pistachio.
Tommy Sledge

What do a cheap hotel and tight jeans have in common?
No ballroom.
M. Rose Pierce

How much does any woman need a man? A test tube full of sperm could be a dad.
Fiona Pitt-Kethley

How many men does it take to screw in a light bulb?
One. Men will screw anything.
Mike Spence

What do we call the fat around the vagina? A woman.
Michel Houellebecq
Platform, 2005

What is man's most effective form of contraceptive?
His personality.
Tania Golightly
Men – can't live with them … can't live with them, 1998

Have you heard about the woman who had sex with a racehorse?
She's now in a stable condition.
Richard Lederer

Rape

A rapist is a rapist, whether he is married to his victim or not.
John Patten

Fascism begins in bed, when a man makes a woman submit to his wishes, forces her to perform acts she doesn't want to perform.
Bernardo Bertolucci

Rape is the only crime in which the victim becomes the accused.
Freda Adler
Sisters in Crime, 1975

Rape is not aggressive sexuality but sexualized aggression.
Audre Lorde
Sister Outsider, 1984

Speaking about rape: even the most fanatic feminists must admit that men are better at it that than women.
Gabrielle Burton
Speech, 29.10.1976

When this judge let a rapist go because the woman had been wearing a miniskirt and so was 'asking for it' I thought, 'Ladies, what we all should do is this: next time we see an ugly guy in the street, shoot him. After all, he knew he was ugly when he left the house. He was asking for it.'
Ellen Cleghorn

Politically, I call it rape whenever a woman has sex and feels violated.
Catharine A. MacKinnon
Feminism Unmodified, 1987

A little romp before penetration is called rape nowadays.
Jef Geeraerts
Gedachten van een linkse bourgeois, 1977

All men are rapists and that's all they are. They rape us with their eyes, their laws and their codes.
Marilyn French
The Women's Room, 1977

Bad judgement and carelessness are not punishable by rape.
Pearl Cleage

Sex and Sport

Some male athletes have breasts I've only dreamed about.
Ruby Wax

When I beat a man at pool, he seems to think he's had his willy chopped off.
Sue Thompson

I haven't had sex in eight months. To be honest, I now prefer to go bowling.
Lil' Kim

Golf is like sex: afterwards you feel you should have scored a little better.
Chris Plumridge
It Can Only Happen to a Golfer, 1999

Good golf is like good sex – the pleasure lies more in the foreplay than the actual scoring.
Sandy Parr
A Little Book of Golf, 2000

Golf and sex are about the only things you can enjoy without being good at.
Jimmy Demaret

Golf is like an 18-year-old girl with big boobs. You know it's wrong but you can't keep away from her.
Val Doonican

Golf, sex, and child-rearing prove that practice does not make perfect.
Paul Dickson
The Official Explanations, 1980

They say that golf has replaced sex. Of course, the men over sixty are saying it.
Milton Berle
More of the Best of Milton Berle's Private Joke File, 1996

Any persons (except players) caught collecting golf balls on this course will be prosecuted and have their balls removed.
Michael Mavor

The golf swing is like sex: you can't be thinking of the mechanics of the act while you're doing it.
Dave Hill

Old golfers never die, they only lose their balls.
Max Hodes
Never Say Die, 1987

Inches make champions.
Vince Lombardi

Being with a woman all night never hurt no professional baseball player. It's staying up all night looking for a woman that does him in.
Casey Stengel

The Vagina

On going out with gynecologists: Never date a man who knows more about your vagina than you do.
Dana Stevens

Men fear the vagina more than women envy the penis.
J.A.M. Mathijsen
Propria Cures, 1975

To have a vagina *and* a point of view in Hollywood is a lethal combination.
Sharon Stone
Empire, June 1992

An erect penis is a sign of power in our culture, but it has virtually no muscles – but the vagina certainly has.
Hilde van der Ploeg

A vagina is a shoe that fits all feet. It is as strong and durable as a boot. It's not the thick penises that make a woman suffer, but the long ones.
Gérard Zwang

Inasmuch as the vagina is the beginning for everybody there is a misunderstanding that it is also the end.
Battus
De Encyclopedie, 1978

The vagina is the eternal 'gap in the market' that can't be filled by any enterprise.
Hans van Straten
De omgevallen boekenkast, 1988

If my vagina could monologue it would ... say: you lying, cheating, hypocritical bastard.
Kathy Lette

And then I saw him and I knew it right away ... it was vaginal contraction at first sight!'
Kees van Kooten and Wim de Bie

There are really not many jobs that actually require a penis or a vagina, and all other occupations should be open to everyone.
Gloria Steinem

I have only one wrinkle and I'm sitting on it.
Jeanne Calment

Quite handy when you have two mouths to answer!
Jean Giraudoux

The truth about the female sex organ: it is a muscle.
Wolinski

Variations

I'm a terrible lover. I've actually given a woman an anti-climax.
Scott Roeben

Whoever allows himself to be whipped, deserves to be whipped.
Leopold von Sacher-Masoch

If it is the dirty element that gives pleasure to the act of lust, then the dirtier it is, the more pleasurable it is bound to be.
Marquis de Sade

Inflatable dolls – the ad says, 'She never has a headache.'
But *you* do, blowing her up.
Robert Schimmel

A woman you take from behind is faceless.
Tomi Ungerer
Vracs, 2000

One necrophiliac to another: 'Don't let it get cold ...'
Kamagurka

The height of despair: a necrophiliac with his pants down at the exit of a crematorium.
Kamagurka

I have tried several varieties of sex. The conventional position makes me claustrophobic. And the others either give me a stiff neck or lockjaw.
Tallulah Bankhead
Tallulah, 1952

The sort of man who seeks extracurricular sex is more often than not a man who is a very poor lay to start with.
Julie Burchill

I had to give up masochism – I was enjoying it too much.
Mel Calman

Whoever said talk is cheap never saw a bill for Phonesex.
Michael Corcoran

I'm not embarrassed about having phone sex. You know what's embarrassing about phone sex is that the neighbours can hear me having sex but they don't see anyone enter or leave my apartment.
Sue Kolinsky

I got sexually desperate, so I called one of those live sex numbers. I got a girl that stuttered. It cost me 1,500 bucks.
Johnny Rizzo

I tried phone sex and it gave me an ear infection.
Richard Lewis

I tried phone sex once. Got my penis stuck in the nine.
Kevin Meaney

Facing our sexual fantasies honestly would tell us a lot about ourselves.
André Guindon

My wife insists on turning off the lights when we make love. That doesn't bother me. It's the hiding that seems so cruel.
Jonathan Katz

I have low self-esteem. When we were in bed together, I would fantasize that I'm someone else.
Richard Lewis

A fella's talking to his priest. He said, 'I gave up sex for Lent … Well, I tried to, but the last day of Lent my wife dropped a can of peaches and when she bent over to pick 'em up, I couldn't help it.'
The priest said, 'That's all right, son, a lot of people give in to temptation.'
He said, 'You're not gonna throw us out of church?'
The priest said no.
He said, 'Well, thank goodness. They threw us out of the supermarket!'
George Lindsey

You know what I say about edible panties? I say, 'If you're drunk enough and your teeth are sharp enough … ANY panties are edible.'
Brian McKim

Let us remember the unfortunate econometrician who, in one of the major functions of his system, had to use a proxy for risk and a dummy for sex.
Fritz Machlup

Sex with a blow-up doll is not as good as advertised.
Norm McDonald

All forms of sexual loving become acceptable if the lovers wear togas or wolfskins.
Naomi Mitchison

My wife only likes to have sex in places where there is a risk of getting caught. Well, I *have* caught her numerous times, in fact.
Brad Osberg

Whenever sexual freedom is sought or achieved, sado-masochism will not be far behind.
Camille Paglia

My classmates would copulate with anything that moved, but I never saw any reason to limit myself.
Emo Philips

Virginity

She lost her virginity in the crowd.
Gabriël Bacri

The problem is that all men want a virgin with the experience of a whore.
Jeanne Moreau

When listening closely to the belly of a virgin at the moment of her menopause, you can hear clearly an enormous cry of despair.
François Cavanna
Les Pensées, 1994

There are women who become virgins again when they make love again.
Willem Elsschot

You can always tell a virgin by the length of her ear-lobes.
Errol Flynn

Virginity is very like a souvenir, sometimes priceless to its owner but, alas, worth much less in the open market.
John B. Keane
The Little Book of John B. Keane, 2000

He said, 'If I'd've known you were a virgin I'd've taken more time.'
She said, 'If I'd've known you had more time I'd've taken my tights off.'
Ellie Laine

When they asked her if, at the age of five, she was a virgin, the Vestal Virgin answered, 'Not yet.'
Tom Lanoye

Sex Miscellany

Friendship between man and woman is impossible because there must be sexual intercourse.
James Joyce
Dubliners, 1914

My next-door neighbour is always bragging about the sex he and his wife have had. As if I hadn't been watching.
Brian Kiley

Sex is the best kept secret in creation. No woman will ever know what it's like to be a man and vice versa.
Rudy Kousbroek

The pleasure of making love increases the indifference felt towards the partner.
Claire Lardinois
Réflexions mauvaises, 1951

You should be able to order sex and pay for it monthly, like laundry.
Philip Larkin

Impotent poets have more time to write poems about love.
Gabriël Laub
Verärgerte Logik, 1969

Impotence in old age has not been a problem. It's like being unchained from a lunatic.
George Melly

If your sexual fantasies were truly of interest to others, they would no longer be fantasies.
Fran Lebowitz

During the process of man's civilization, his genitals remained semi-wild.
Goedele Liekens

Good sex should involve laughter. Because it is, you know, funny.
Stephanie Lucas

Men get such brilliant ideas during sex because they are plugged into a genius.
Mary Lynch

If sex were not pleasurable only wanted children would be born.
Amanda Marteleur

In reality, despite the daydreams of many men, females rarely force sexual intercourse on males.
C.H. McCaghy
Deviant Behaviour, 1976

The best thing about being in a relationship is having someone right there to do it with when you're horny.
Jenny McCarthy

My wife thinks fuckin' and cookin' are two towns in China.
John McNaughton
Mad Dog and Glory, 1993

What you don't see is far more erotic than what you see.
Deepa Mehta
Ms., November 1997

It doesn't matter how often a couple have sex as long as it is the same number for both of them.
Marian Mills

There are two things no man will admit he cannot do well: drive and make love.
Stirling Moss

Monogamy leaves a lot to be desired.
Francis Blanche
Pensées, répliques et anecdotes, 1996

The only time children are not a problem is when we are making them.
Patrick Sébastien

The most shameless women are those with the most beautiful behinds.
Réjean Ducharme

Today, when a woman sleeps with a man she's not necessarily trying to get him – she's just trying to get through to him.
Cristina Odone
The Observer, 2.12.2001

You know more about a man in one night in bed than you do in months of conversation. In the sack, they can't cheat.
Edith Piaf

It is not sex that gives the pleasure, but the lover.
Marge Piercy

God gave women buttocks because sooner or later they have to walk away from us, and at least this way there's some consolation.
Joe Quigley

The only premarital thing girls don't do these days is cooking.
Omar Sharif

Why should we take advice on sex from the Pope? If he knows anything about it, he shouldn't.
George Bernard Shaw

They say the best exercise takes place in the bedroom. I believe it, because that's where I get the most resistance.
Jeff Shaw

My regret in life is that I haven't had enough sex.
John Betjeman

There is an old saying in my family: push sex out of the front door and it will come back through the plughole.
Lynne Truss

I thank God I was raised Catholic, so sex will always be dirty.
John Waters

There are no frigid women, there are only inexperienced men.
George Lombard Kelly
Sexual Relations in Marriage, 1954

For their twenty-fifth wedding anniversary, they gave each other inscribed tombstones. Hers read 'Here lies my wife, cold as usual' while his read 'Here lies my husband, stiff at last.'
Jack South

A man's sexuality goes through three stages: tri-weekly, try-weekly, and try-weakly.
Maxim Drabon

If there's a worse insult I don't know it. I have just been told by my friend Gladys that she'd trust her husband to spend an evening alone with me.
Marjorie Proops

It's lucky that people's arses don't have swing-doors.
Johan Anthierens
De lange weg tot jezelf, 1977

Sex in the hands of public educators is not a pretty thing.
Carol Black
The Wonder Years, 1988

My lover asked me if I wanted to have children. I told her I didn't know, but we should keep trying.
Suzy Berger

Things you'll never hear a woman say: 'My, what an attractive scrotum!'
Patricia Arquette

If it is not erotic, it is not interesting.
   Fernando Arrabal

To write badly about sex is filthy.
   Fernand Auwera
   Allerlei redenen om te zwijgen, 1974

Sex discrimination need not stifle your opportunities for career advancement if you are flexible enough to consider a sex change.
   Pat Paulsen

Every woman keeps a fortune between her legs.
   Honoré de Balzac
   Pensées, Sujets, Fragments, 1833

I once made love for an hour and fifteen minutes, but it was the night the clocks are set ahead.
   Garry Shandling

Nurses are easy ... because they know where everything is.
   Pete Barbutti

It isn't premarital sex if you have no intention of getting married.
   Matt Barry

There's nothing wrong with a person's sex life that the right psychoanalyst can't exaggerate.
   Gerald Horton Bath

Erotic is when you use a feather, kinky is when you use the whole chicken. Perverted is chicken soup for dinner guests the next day.
   C. Haynes

People today say you cannot be happy unless your sex life is happy. That makes about as much sense as saying you cannot be happy unless your golf life is happy.
   Evelyn Waugh

If it weren't for pickpockets I'd have no sex life at all.
Rodney Dangerfield

I had to go to analysis. They told me I had an unresolved Oedipus complex, which, according to them, meant I want to sleep with my mother. Which is preposterous. My father doesn't even want to sleep with my mother.
Dennis Wolfberg

As for Mama, she never recovered completely from the combined shocks of sex and childbirth.
Vicki Baum
And Life Goes On, 1932

In my days, hot pants were something we had, not wore.
Bette Davis

Those hot pants of hers were so damned tight, I could hardly breathe.
Benny Hill
The Benny Hill Show, 1984

The miniskirt enables young ladies to run faster, and because of it, they may have to.
John V. Lindsay

The miniskirt – never in the history of fashion has so little material been raised so high to reveal so much that needs to be covered so badly.
Cecil Beaton

The family was shocked when my sister announced that she was going to the police academy. We thought that she was heterosexual.
Dwight York

Take me as I am
or otherwise in the dark.
Marcel Beekman
True Love

I've never turned over a fig leaf that didn't have a price tag on the other side.
Saul Bellow

I went to a meeting for premature ejaculators. I left early.
Jack Benny

I was a man trapped in a woman's body. That was before I was born, of course.
Mike Bent

Sexual harassment on the job is not a problem for virtuous women.
Phyllis Schlafly

Women who complain of sexual harassment are, more often than not, revoltingly ugly.
Auberon Waugh

'You worked in an office once didn't you, Jill?' a feminist once asked earnestly. 'Did men ever harass you?' 'Yes,' I replied, 'but not nearly enough.'
Jilly Cooper

Aids obliges people to think of sex as having, possibly, the direst consequences: suicide. Or murder.
Susan Sontag
Tonight Show, 14.8.1989

Men are impatient and that's precisely why the zip was invented.
Senta Berger

When people say, 'You're breaking my heart', they do in fact usually mean that you're breaking their genitals.
Jeffrey Bernard

'Don't worry 'bout yer old genitals, lad,' said the old man, 'they'll stand up fer themselves.'
Spike Milligan
Puckoon, 1963

We weren't having an affair. He was just lying on top of me to get the creases out of my negligée.
Victoria Wood

People always talk of a love affair as if lovers spent all their time in bed.
Anthony Powell

I date this girl for two years – and then the nagging starts: 'I wanna know your name.'
Mike Binder

A woman that is easy to seduce is also easily lost.
Willy Birgel

There is something rather greedy about being bisexual.
Toon Verhoeven
Terzijde, 1990

If bisexuals were hermaphrodite, life would be a lot easier for them.
Yvan Audouard
Les Pensées, 1991

Happy are the bisexuals who can look the whole of mankind in the eye with love.
Philippe Bouvard
Maximes au minimum, 1984

I'm bisexual. When ever I want sex I can buy it.
Eric Idle

I'm glad I'm not bisexual. I couldn't stand being rejected by men as well as women.
Bernard Manning

Bisexuality is not so much a cop-out as a fearful compromise.
Jill Johnston
Lesbian Nation, 1973

A 'Bay Area Bisexual' told me I didn't quite coincide with either of her desires.
Woody Allen
The Lunatic's Tale, 1986

What annoys me most about Catholics is the way they constantly talk about sex, like we atheists talk about God.
Heinrich Böll

Women often complain about too little, never about too much.
Guillaume Bouchet
Les Sérées, 1584

The 1950s was the most sexually frustrated decade ever. Ten years of foreplay.
Lily Tomlin

Anyone who eats three meals a day should understand why cookbooks outsell sex books three to one.
L.M. Boyd

I've been in more laps than a napkin.
Mae West
I'm No Angel, 1933

An erection is a mysterious thing. There's always that fear, each time one goes, that you won't be seeing it again.
Kirk Douglas
The Ragman's Son, 1988

Morning erection: If only I could get that in the evening.
Jean Blaute
Flemish television, 28.4.2003

'Obesity causes erection problems,' it said in the newspaper. Actually, fat people do have erections, it's just that they can't see them.
Raf Coppens
Het Nieuwsblad, 11.9.2004

I suspect
There would be more poems
About sex
If it rhymed with more than
Pecks
Necks
Erects and ejects.
Lynn Peters

When she asked, 'Is that a roll of quarters in your pocket, or are you just glad to see me?' we both just had to laugh, because, being a peepshow girl, it really didn't matter to her either way.
Brad Simanek

Sex may not be everything, everything has to do with sex.
C. Buddingh
Niets spreekt vanzelf, 1981

Have you heard about the deaf gynecologist?
He had to learn to read lips.
Richard Lederer

If it's wet, dry it. If it's dry, wet it. Congratulations, you are now a gynecologist.
Patrick Murray

Sometimes I wonder if my gynecologist is charging me too much.
Andy Pierson

I'm a hypochondriac. At least that's what my gynecologist keeps telling me.
Gregg Rogell

I went to the gynaecologist. She goes, 'God, you're clean. You are so clean. How do you stay so clean?' I said, 'It's easy, I have a woman come in twice a week.'
Karen Ripley

The only thing that can make a woman feel lonelier than a vibrator can make her feel is a man.
Isha Elafi

When they found out their wives were attending a sex-toy party, the husbands refused to go and pick them up, and instead left them to their own devices.
James Pierce

Sex appeal is in you, not in your blouse.
Claudia Cardinale
Humo, 3.12.1992

She was a blonde. A blonde to make a bishop kick a hole in a stained-glass window.
Raymond Chandler
Farewell, My Lovely, 1940

There is no more exquisite combination than that of innocence and sex appeal.
Marcello Mastroianni

A man's sex appeal is made up of power, money and a sharp perfume – in that order.
Vivien Mellish

Sex is interesting, but it's not totally important. I mean it's not even as important as excretion. A man can go seventy years without a piece of ass, but he can die in a week without a bowel movement.
Charles Bukowski
Notes of a Dirty Old Man, 1969

I am constantly amazed when I talk to young people to learn how much they know about sex and how little about soap.
Billie Burke

Apparently, women need to feel loved to have sex. Men need to have sex to feel loved. How do we ever get started?
Billy Connolly

It's hard to be devil-may-care when there are pleats in your derrière.
Judith Viorst

Keep looking at my eyes, dahling. My arse is like an accordion.
Tallulah Bankhead
Tallulah, 1952

If someone had told me years ago that sharing a sense of humour was so vital to partnerships, I could have avoided a lot of sex.
Kate Beckinsale

Frequent sex has its ups and downs.
Anthony Cacchillo

When a woman becomes a scholar there is usually something wrong with her sexual organs.
Friedrich Nietzsche

Sex is not something we do, it is something we are.
Mary Calderone

The only talk I've had on sex was from an embarrassed headmaster about the reproduction of lupins. I'm as ready as can be if ever I fall in love with a lupin.
Miles Kington

The only sex education I got at school was just as we were about to leave, a master said, 'Don't fornicate in Old Etonian braces.' It was as good advice as any.
Robert Mason

The sexual closet is bigger than you think.
Pat Califia
ZG, 1982

It's just handy to fuck your best friend.
John Lennon
on Yoko Ono

To marry – a worse bargain. Available sex against not being allowed to fart in bed.
Tom Stoppard
Arcadia, 1993

I don't mind where people make love, so long as they don't do it in the street and frighten the horses.
Mrs Patrick Campbell
The Duchess of Jermyn Street, 1984

Thank God a soul has no buttocks.
Remco Campert
Luister goed naar wat ik verzwijg, 1976

Perhaps men could be divided into two kinds – those who take their watches off, and those who leave them on.
Charlotte Chandler
The Ultimate Seduction, 1984

Learning and sex until rigor mortis!
Maggie Kuhn

Did I sleep with her? Not a wink, Reverend Father, not a wink.
Brendan Behan

Sex can be a dirty postcard, a cane, a sauna, clothes on a washing line, a locked drawer, an address book, cash on the mantelpiece, a gentleman's lavatory, a frantic exposure, the consummation of love, a peeping Tom.
Robert Morley
Responsible Gentleman, 1966

My parents were very wise. They preferred to have me learn about sex from my friends in the gutter – which is still by far the best way.
Al Capp
The First Time, 1975

Yes, you are the first one, and I'll tell you more: you are the first one who believes it.
Alfred Capus
Notes et Pensées, 1926

If a woman says: This is my first time, it means: This is my first time with you.
Lorene Machado
Was It Something I Said, 1996

I hate hearing complaints after sex. Especially the criminal ones.
Dwight York

I'm not a good lover, but at least I'm fast.
Drew Carey

She was a lovely girl. Our courtship was fast and furious – I was fast and she was furious.
Max Kauffman

A woman will sooner show her arse than her heart.
Honoré de Balzac
Pensées, Sujets, Fragments, 1833

There's an inverse relationship between availablity and desirability.
Philip Simborg

Forbidden fruits create many jams.
Suzann Schiewer

For men obsessed with women's underwear, a course in washing, ironing and mending is recommended.
Charlotte Perkins Gilman

You can always recognise a woman by her underwear.
Hugues C. Pernath

I've always thought that lingerie was a nice gift, especially for a woman to whom you're very close.
Something tells me, though, that Grandma would've preferred slippers.
Kurt R. Matis

Little kids buy cereal the way grown men buy lingerie – they will buy things they care nothing about just to get the toy that is inside.
Jeff Foxworthy

Two eyes that see a beautiful behind are worth less than the one finger that is allowed to touch it.
Professor Choron

Erogenous zones are either everywhere or nowhere.
Joseph Heller
Good as Gold, 1979

A wet dream is no illusion.
Rinus Ferdinandusse
Stukjes in de kraag, 1965

Bad arse, bad character.
Jan Cremer
Credo's van Cremer, 1994

The man was fragile and small, barely five feet tall. The woman on the other hand was almost twice as tall and so fat. Their relationship made me think of erotic mountaineering.
Simon Carmiggelt
Het klinkt soms wel aardig, 1982

I'd rather share my bed with a woman who looks like a man, than with a man who looks like a woman.
Wolinski
La Morale, 1992

A woman broke up with me and sent me pictures of her and her new boyfriend in bed together. Solution? I sent them to her dad.
Christopher Case

He always talks to his wife after making love – if she happens to be there.
Joey Adams
Strictly For Laughs, 1981

He is very small, but in bed that doesn't matter.
Marie Chevreuse

Impression of a one-night stand: Oooh. Ahhhhh. Get out.
Andrew Dice Clay

Women want men with flat stomachs and fat wallets. My sex life still hasn't recovered from getting it backwards.
Derek Cockram

The whole joy of sex-with-love is that there are no rules.
Alex Comfort
The Joy of Sex, 1986

I do not think sex is the most important thing. The most important thing is to multiply certain things by two.
Herman de Coninck
Een aangename postumiteit, 2004

I met my wife at a singles bar. We were both very surprised.
Brian Conley

Disapproving grandmother: 'In my day, if a girl didn't have anything to wear she stayed at home.'
John Conway

We'll have a counseling session later on, and you can tell us how you first found out that you were a heterosexual.
Kaz Cooke

Sex is not imaginary, but it is not quite real either.
Mason Cooley
City Aphorisms, Eighth Selection, 1991

All too many men still believe that what feels good to them is automatically what feels good to a woman.
Shere Hite
The Hite Report, 1976

Only death goes deeper than sex.
Mason Cooley
City Aphorisms, Eighth Selection, 1991

Making love within a marriage means that if the phone goes you sometimes answer it.
Mavis Cheek
The Sex Life of My Aunt, 2002

Sex when you're married is like going to a 7-Eleven. There is not as much variety, but at three in the morning, it's always there.
Carol Leifer

Sex was for men, and marriage, like lifeboats, was for women and children.
Carrie Fisher
Surrender the Pink, 1990

✈ I don't see what the big deal is about same-sex marriages. Every married couple I know has the same sex all the time.
Jim Rosenberg

My mother-in-law broke up my marriage. My wife came home from work one day and found me in bed with her.
Lenny Bruce
The Essential Lenny Bruce, 1970

Sex is the great amateur art. The professional, male or female, is frowned upon. He or she misses the whole point and spoils the show.
David Cort

Every time you think you've been screwed by publishers in every possible way, you meet one who has read the *Kama Sutra*.
Cathy Crimmins

If sex is technical, then women are not yet machines.
Geertrui Daem
Een vader voor Elizabeth, 1994

Many women open their legs to allow their brain to breathe.
Frédéric Dard
Les Pensées de San-Antonio, 1996

The Law Society prohibits sex between lawyers and their clients to prevent clients from being billed twice for essentially the same service.
Alan Davies

My wife is a sex object. Every time I ask for sex, she objects.
Les Dawson
The Les Dawson Joke Book, 1979

The veil reduces a woman to a sexual object.
Chahdortt Djavann
P-magazine, 24.2.2004

If I believed in casual sex, I'd have stayed married.
Marsha Doble

Everybody lies about sex.
Robert A. Heinlein
Time Enough for Love, 1973

When you don't have any money, the problem is food.
When you have money, the problem is sex.
When you have both, it's health.
J.P. Donleavy
The Ginger Man, 1955

Nobody, including the Supreme Court, knows what obscenity is.
Norman Dorsen

Sex without eroticism is no more than contact between two skin-owners.
Marguerite Duras

No woman needs intercourse; few women escape it.
Andrea Dworkin
Right-Wing Women, 1978

If God didn't want you to have sex, he would have changed his name so you wouldn't be able to scream it out when you came.
Lou Eisen

If God intended that the genitals were more important than the brain, he would've put a skull over the genitals.
Mel Brooks

Making love. Even if they invented something funnier, I would still keep on doing it.
Edouard Elias

Birth, copulation and death.
That's all the facts when you come to brass tacks;
Birth, copulation and death.
T.S. Eliot
Sweeney Agonistes, 1932

Sex is an extraordinary way of bringing babies into the world. I don't know how God thought of it.
Winston Churchill

She had heard that men only wanted one thing, but had forgotten for the moment what it was.
Barbara Pym

Marriage – compared with going to bed with each other, this is a child's game.
J.A. Emmens
Gedachten en aforismen, 1980

No man can ever be friends with a woman that he finds attractive. He always wants to have sex with her.
Nora Ephron
When Harry Met Sally, 1989

Many a beautiful girl ruins her charm by using the four-letter words – like 'don't' and 'stop'.
Evan Esar

I would read *Playboy* magazine more often, but my glasses keep steaming over.
George Burns

There's a new edition of *Playboy* magazine designed for married men. Every month the centerfold is the same picture.
Mary Crowley

If a man says: I read *Playboy* for the articles, it means: I read the phone book for the pictures.
Lorene Machado
Was It Something I Said, 1996

Long before *Playboy*, woman was not the sum of her parts: her parts were her sum.
Marya Mannes

One important thing came out of the Persian Gulf War. They now have a *Playboy* channel in Kuwait where women do naughty things like work and vote.
Denise Munro

My boyfriend used to say, 'I read *Playboy* for the articles.' Right, and I go to shopping malls for the music.
Rita Rudner

She would be a nymphomaniac if only they could calm her down a little.
Judy Garland

Nymphomaniac. You can't have all the guys in the world, but you can try.
Claude Angeli

Nobody in their right mind would call me a nymphomaniac. I only sleep with good-looking men.
Fiona Pitt-Kethley

You were born with your legs apart. They'll send you to your grave in a Y-shaped coffin.
Joe Orton
What the Butler Saw, 1969

She's been in more motel rooms than the Bible.
Joan Rivers
The Life and Hard Times of Heidi Abromowitz, 1984

Your body isn't just your temple, it's also your holy brothel.
Eurydice

Sex suppressed will go berserk,
But it keeps us all alive.
It's a wonderful change from wives and work
And it ends at half past five.
Gavin Ewart
Office Friendships, 1966

The rallying cry for my sexual manifesto is: Cocks and pussies of the world, unite; you have nothing to lose but your hang-ups.
Keith Ferreira

Sex is hereditary. If your parents never had it, chances are you won't either.
Joseph Fischer

My feelings about sex? Sex is part of nature and I go along with nature.
Marilyn Monroe
Marilyn Monroe In Her Own Words, 1990

Men want a woman whom they can turn on and off like a light switch.
Ian Fleming
Life of Ian Fleming, 1966

Big women are sexier – we pump more oestrogen, have higher sex drives and fantasize more.
Dawn French

Some women are sexy and some only act sexy.
Marilyn French
The Women's Room, 1977

Sometimes a cigar is just a cigar.
Sigmund Freud

In love the paradox occurs that two beings become one and yet remain two.
Erich Fromm
The Sane Society, 1955

Personally I know nothing about sex because I have always been married.
Zsa Zsa Gabor
The Observer, 16.8.1987

You also want to have a high degree of sexuality in the appeal … cigarettes are essentially very close to a sexual product.
Fritz Gahagan

As long as a person does not give up sex, sex does not give up a person.
Gabriel Garcia Marquez
Love in the Time of Cholera, 1985

Eroticism can only flourish in a climate of attention and concentration.
Jef Geeraerts
Gedachten van een linkse bourgeois, 1977

Girls are always running through my mind. They don't dare walk.
Andy Gibb

Sex? I'd rather have a Bounty any day. It tastes better, it's cheaper and you don't have to feel bad when you forgot to use a condom.
Ronald Giphart
Giph, 1993

As soon as I get home I'm going to rip my wife's bra off. The elastic is killing me.
Roy Brown

Sex for a fat man is much ado about puffing.
Jackie Gleason

A woman tries to get all she can out of a man, and a man tries to get all he can into a woman.
Isaac Goldberg

Having sex with your husband is like getting an injection at the doctor's.
It's all over before you feel a thing.
Tania Golightly
Men – can't live with them … can't live with them, 1998

The average male thinks about sex every eleven minutes while he's awake.
Patrick Greene

You go to jail for doin' something normal. Ain't no law against peein' in public. They get you for indecent exposure. As long as you pee and don't zip your pants down, that's normal.
Dick Gregory

Sex just hasn't been the same since women started enjoying it.
Lewis Grizzard
The Wit and Wisdom of Lewis Grizzard, 1993

When sex is involved the anatomy loses its innocence.
Benoîte Groult

They're working on Viagra for women. Are they crazy? That's been around for hundreds of years – it's called cash.
Alonzo Boden

If I marry again at my age, I'll go on honeymoon to Viagra Falls.
George Burns

Apparently Viagra can be very bad for the eyes. So it's not love that makes you blind – just sex.
Geert Hoste

The trouble with Viagra is that it can keep you stiff: permanently.
David Letterman

The judge said he was afraid that my frequent thefts of Viagra have made me a hardened criminal.
James Bernard Murphy

I only take Viagra when I'm with more than one woman.
Jack Nicholson

The joyfulness of a man prolongeth his days. (Psalms)
Viagra does the same for his nights.
Scott Roeben

I just took two Viagra; now I'm as hard as Chinese algebra.
Robin Williams

I've got to stop taking Viagra because I can't zip up my trousers.
Richard Harris

Amoebas at the start
Were not complex;
They tore themselves apart
And started sex.
   Arthur Guiterman

Sex should not be taught in schools, unless the teacher really wants to learn.
   Morty Gunty

Any woman who thinks the way to a man's heart is through his stomach is aiming about ten inches too high.
   Adrienne E. Gusoff

Good lovers have known for centuries that the hand is probably the primary sex organ.
   Eleanor Hamilton
   San Francisco Chronicle, 1978

I believe in making the world safe for our children, but not our children's children, because I don't think children should be having sex.
   Jack Handey
   Deep Thoughts, 1992

When our organs have been transplanted
And the new ones made happy to lodge in us,
Let us pray one wish be granted –
We retain our zones erogenous.
   E.Y. Harburg

Sex and beauty are inseparable,
Like life and consciousness.
And the intelligence which goes
With sex and beauty,
Is intuition.
   D.H. Lawrence

Sexuality was previously unknown, or unrecognized, it was discovered accidently on a rainy day when two feminists and a gay clinical psychologist were cleaning out a closet.
Edmund H. Volkart
The Angel's Dictionary, 1986

Whatever else can be said about sex, it cannot be called a dignified performance.
Helen Lawrenson
Whistling Girl, 1978

Books on sex can give you a terrible inferiority complex.
Mike Harding
The Armchair Anarchist's Almanac, 1981

For a woman there is nothing more erotic than being understood.
Molly Haskell

There were nine buttons on her nightgown, but she could only fascinate.
Homer Haynes

A man who can't kiss can't fuck.
Cynthia Heimel
Sex Tips for Girls, 1983

Everything's either
concave or -vex,
so whatever you dream
will be something with sex.
Piet Hein
Grooks, 1966

⋆ Premenstrual Syndrome: just before their periods women behave the way men do all the time.
Robert A. Heinlein
Time Enough for Love, 1973

When sex isn't thrilling any more it becomes repulsive. There is nothing in between.
Benoîte Groult

I was very sheltered growing up. I knew nothing about sex. My mother said: 'Sex is a dirty, disgusting thing you save for somebody you love.'
Carol Henry

I wonder why it is, that young men are always cautioned against bad girls. Anyone can handle a bad girl. It's the good girls men should be warned against.
F. Hugh Herbert
The Moon is Blue, 1953

My grandmother had twelve children.
She had no time for sex.
Toon Hermans
Elke dag een treetje, 1990

I know I must be really good in bed, 'cause women always ask me if there's any possible way I could make it last longer.
Bill Hewins

I was pretty old before I had my first sexual experience. The reason was that I was born by Caesarian section and had no frame of reference.
Jeff Hilton

I'm suggesting we call sex something else, and it should include everything from kissing to sitting close together.
Shere Hite
The Hite Report, 1976

The only alliance I would make with the Women's Liberation Movement is in bed.
Abbie Hoffman

I hate the saying 'nice guys finish last'. Every nice guy I've dated finished first and didn't last.
Kate Hoffman

She said she would scream for help.
I told her I didn't need any help.
Bob Hope

Sex becomes an obsession for those who always think about it but never practise it.
Michel Houellebecq
Humo, 12.10.1999

Sex is a wonderful experience.
Especially with another person.
Dom Irrera

I'd rather she'd used me for sex. Using me for my mind really bothered me.
Carl Jacobs

Next time I'm not just having an epidural for the birth – I'm having one for the conception as well.
Sally James

 Heterosexuality isn't normal – it's just common.
Derek Jarman
The Observer, 6.3.1994

I know nothing about platonic love except that it is not to be found in the works of Plato.
Edgar Jepson

Platonic love exists, but it only occurs with couples.
Emanuel Wertheimer

New research shows that the more sex a man has, the more he wants. Not only that, the research also shows the less sex a man has, the more he wants.
Conan O'Brien

A healthy sex life. Best thing in the world for a woman's voice.
Leontyne Price

I did not sleep. I never do when I am over-happy, over-unhappy, or in bed with a strange man.
Edna O'Brien

The bed of Eros is festooned with amazing flowers.
Henri-Floris Jespers

I have never liked sex. I do not think I ever will. It seems just the opposite of love.
Marilyn Monroe
Marilyn Monroe In Her Own Words, 1990

Kids – they're not easy, but there has to be some penalty for sex.
Bill Maher

Girls got balls. They're just a little higher up, that's all.
Joan Jett

They usually talk about 'pains in the heart', when all they mean really is tormented testicles.
Pierre-Robert Leclercq
Mes catins, Les Belles Lettres, Paris 2005